To my mom and my daughter, this one is for you

Sarees

stories in six yards

KALIKA KEKKAR

Edited by Vaishali Bhat

Printed by Kalika Kekkar, in the United States of America

First printing edition 2022.
Contact: SareeRocks4@gmail.com
ISBN: 978-0-578-28954-0

Table of contents

BLOUSE
PALLU
BORDER
BORDER

A word on sarees

Sarees are traditional garments worn in India and many other countries in South Asia. A little bit of orientation is due to those readers who may be unfamiliar with this fascinating garment. For those who know about sarees, this section will be a quick breeze-through.

To describe very simply, a saree is a single, continuous piece of unstitched fabric. While sarees can be of variable length, the most widely used version today is typically six yards in length and forty-four inches in width, the same size fitting anyone and everyone. The basic three sections of a saree would be its base, its two long ***borders***, and its end-piece, called the *pallu*. When a saree is draped, the base is wrapped around the waist of the wearer, the upper border is tucked in to hold the saree in place while the lower border is visible at the bottom. The ***pallu*** is the loose end-piece that is draped over the shoulder (again in multiple ways). Given that the *pallu* and the borders are the most visible parts of the saree, not surprisingly, they are the most decorated too. In the most commonly seen fashions of recent times, a saree is typically paired with a *choli* (cropped top or a blouse) on the torso and held in place with a thin, slender petticoat inside.

While one single piece of cloth, a saree is a fashion statement like none other, defined by its make, material, design, way of draping and accessories. No one is like another; and the same saree worn in different ways with different accessories will look different, making it a beautiful way to express, adorn and array feminine beauty.

How to use this book

This book is for everyone, from first-time saree enthusiasts to lifelong saree lovers and everyone in between. Those who love to see sarees but don't know much about them would definitely learn a lot from it, but also those who know a lot will learn some new things for sure.

Sarees are so diverse and variegated based on weaving techniques, design patterns, and core features, that they can easily fill multiple volumes like this. This book focuses on twenty-one saree types, each described in a chapter dedicated to it. I have chosen these sarees with care, so as to represent as many different states or provinces of India as I could. The name of each chapter contains the name of the saree type, as well as the state it originates from.

Non-English words used in the book

Needless to say, this is such a native Indian topic that it is impossible to translate every term. The reader will encounter several words that are therefore not English words. These are italicized so the reader knows these are from a different language; also, they are spelt phonetically to ensure the reader knows how to pronounce them. Some terms are repeated very often in the book because they are very freely used in the context of sarees. Here are some of them along with descriptions of what they mean and refer to.

Resham literally means silk. In sarees, the word is often used to describe silk thread embroidery or designs woven in a saree.

Zari is the shiny gold or silver decorative thread used for the embellishment in most silk saree weaving to create intricate patterns and rich looks. It is made by twisting a flattened metallic strip, traditionally made of fine gold or silver or metalized polyester film, on a core yarn of silk, viscose, cotton or other artificial yarns.

Butti refers to a small motif used for small designs strewn over a large part of the fabric. It may be a single flower, droplet or similar motif.

Butta is a medium to larger sized motif compared with the butti. Sarees are often embellished with *butti* or *butta* in *zari* or *resham* work in the base of the fabric.

Foreword

"Can you edit my book for me?"was the question that Kalika had just asked me on the phone. In that infinitesimal fraction of a second in which I paused in surprise, fleeting doubts crossed my mind. While I love writing and have been publishing blogs, I had never done an editing assignment yet. Also, the task of editing a whole book when working full time seemed daunting. Yet, the answer to Kalika's question came almost instinctively and instantaneously, "Yes, of course, I will be delighted to!".

The saree has been the garment of the Indian woman from as far back as civilization has existed in the country. A saree is just a six to nine yard-long continuous strip of fabric, a metre or so in width, that a woman drapes around her body. But when draped, it is a gorgeous garment, charmingly and elegantly feminine, with a touch of mystique to it. Add to it the extensive variety of designs, material and styles, and the flexibility in draping and accessorising that a saree offers, and you have an apparel almost unmatched in the fashion possibilities it presents.

The saree is not just a garment, it is a part of the culture and ethos of India, a fashion that's simultaneously traditional and trendy, and can be easily flexed to look fabulous for any occasion, body type and budget. No wonder it has captured the imagination of Indian women from time immemorial to this day. Sarees are worn in India on any and every occasion, the mundane and the special, the formal and the informal. Sarees are the centre of fashion especially in traditional and religious functions, and are favoured gifts on special occasions.

I love sarees. I grew up seeing my beautiful mother, a saree-lover herself, always immaculately dressed in one of her lovely drapes. Like her, I fell into eternal love with sarees – I love seeing them, touching them, wearing them, buying them, whether for myself or someone else. Being involved in a book on sarees was therefore right up my alley. But there was more to the decision.

Kalika and I have been close friends for more than three decades. I had been keenly observing her growing passion for sarees, leading to serious research. Research and making connections have always been Kalika's big strengths. She dug deep into the topic, connecting with weavers and experts, learning about different types, their origins and evolution, culminating into a series of blogs. A bunch of us, her saree-lover friends whom she had brought together, actively discussed sarees and her blogs, sharing opinions, pictures and information. The idea of a coffee table book on sarees was floated by Kalika somewhere in those conversations, a dream we all shared with her. When she asked me to edit this book, it all came together for me – my passion for writing, my love for sarees, and my wish for a dear friend to realise her dream. How could I say no?

Once we started, things just flowed. As my first editing project, this was a learning experience for me. For each saree type, there was a lot of information Kalika had amassed, along with a personal story. I had to understand all these ingredients and then put them together. We worked closely together, to ensure that the final articles fully represent Kalika's detailed work and her personal memories - her research in my words, her stories in my voice. Like me, many other friends worked on it in different ways and in different capacities. This book is therefore, as much our tribute to sarees as it is an expression of our love and respect for each other as friends.

Irrespective of the intensity of the reader's interest in sarees, this book will be a pleasurable read, as it weaves in information while telling interesting stories and showing beautiful pictures, exactly like a coffee-table book should. Readers with a light interest in sarees can enjoy the pictures and stories more, while those with a higher level of interest can also get enough detail without feeling bombarded with too much, to feel equipped to identify saree types by looking at them. I can vouch for that from my personal experience. All in all, the reader will enjoy this read.

I dedicate my contributions towards this book to my mother, who instilled and nurtured in me a love for sarees and for writing; to Kalika, whose friendship I treasure; and to the saree-weavers in India who keep this art alive.

- Vaishali Bhat

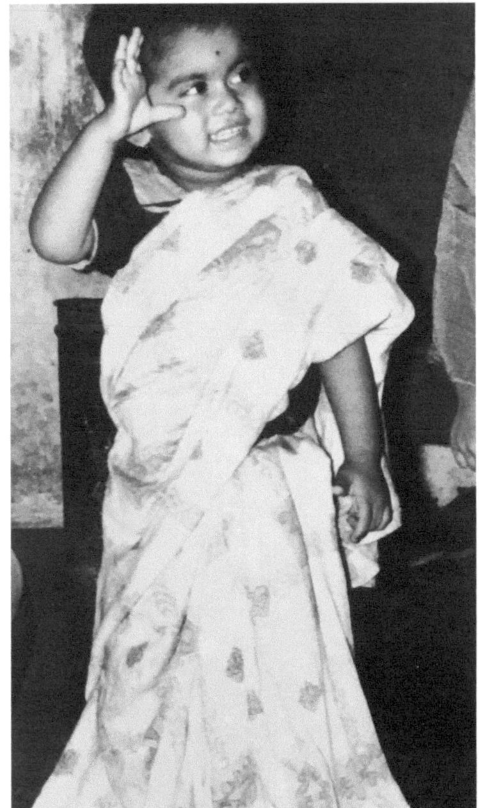

Three Generations
From the left : My mother and my grandmothers at my 4th birthday celebration

Above
Top Left : I am dressed in a saree at age 2
Top Right : My daughter, dressed in a saree at age 2

Introduction

I don't remember my very first moment of fascination with a saree, it was very early in my life. I grew up seeing sarees all around me; after all, it was the everyday dress of the Indian woman when I was growing up. Yet in my mind, the saree is associated with my grandmother. The time I spent with her is fondly wrapped into bundles of loving memories in my mind; maybe the love I have for her got projected and then inextricably connected to the garment she was always wrapped in, which always struck me as beautiful and warm, just like her. And so, my love for sarees comes from and because of my grandmother, and I dedicate this work as an ode to her.

I had a beautiful childhood in Mumbai, in the midst of my immediate and extended family. My grandma and my mom have been pivotal influences in shaping my mind and personality. I would tag along with them and hover around them as a little girl, often latching on literally to their *pallu* (the loose end of a saree hanging over the shoulder of the wearer) as they went about their chores. I knew most of their sarees very well, definitely the regular daily wear ones. And I also knew the ones that came out on special occasions; I distinctly remember the fondness with which they would neatly fold and unfold them, often over discussions about sarees. These conversations were always interesting; I enjoyed them very much, and realized much later in life that they were training my eye and my mind to discern good craftsmanship. As I grew up, I started helping them in the chore of folding sarees; I devised a smart trick when I was about eight, where I would stand on the bed so that I could hold their sarees tall & vertically straight, as I learnt from them how to fold them meticulously. Sarees used to be a mainstay of many family conversations. Family functions were made more fun with saree-shopping trips, which I often joined and looked forward to, as I loved looking at the variety of weaves, designs, fabrics I saw.

Thus started my love affair with sarees, to be honest, quite unbeknownst to me. My admiration and pride for my mom and grandma's sarees continued and grew with time. They didn't have large collections, but every saree they owned was chosen with careful consideration and a lot of analysis of the craft behind it, and then loved and cared for forever. I did wear sarees on special occasions, yet my love for them was not so apparent, even to me. Many of my friends and cousins, who were also saree-lovers, wore their love much more on their sleeve, both literally and figuratively - they wore sarees at every possible occasion, they bought new sarees regularly. I was nowhere in that league. I got sarees as gifts and wore them once in a while, but my love and passion for them, while intrinsic, stayed more in the background, as other worldly priorities took precedence. Yet it endured, and lasted through all the other changes that happened.

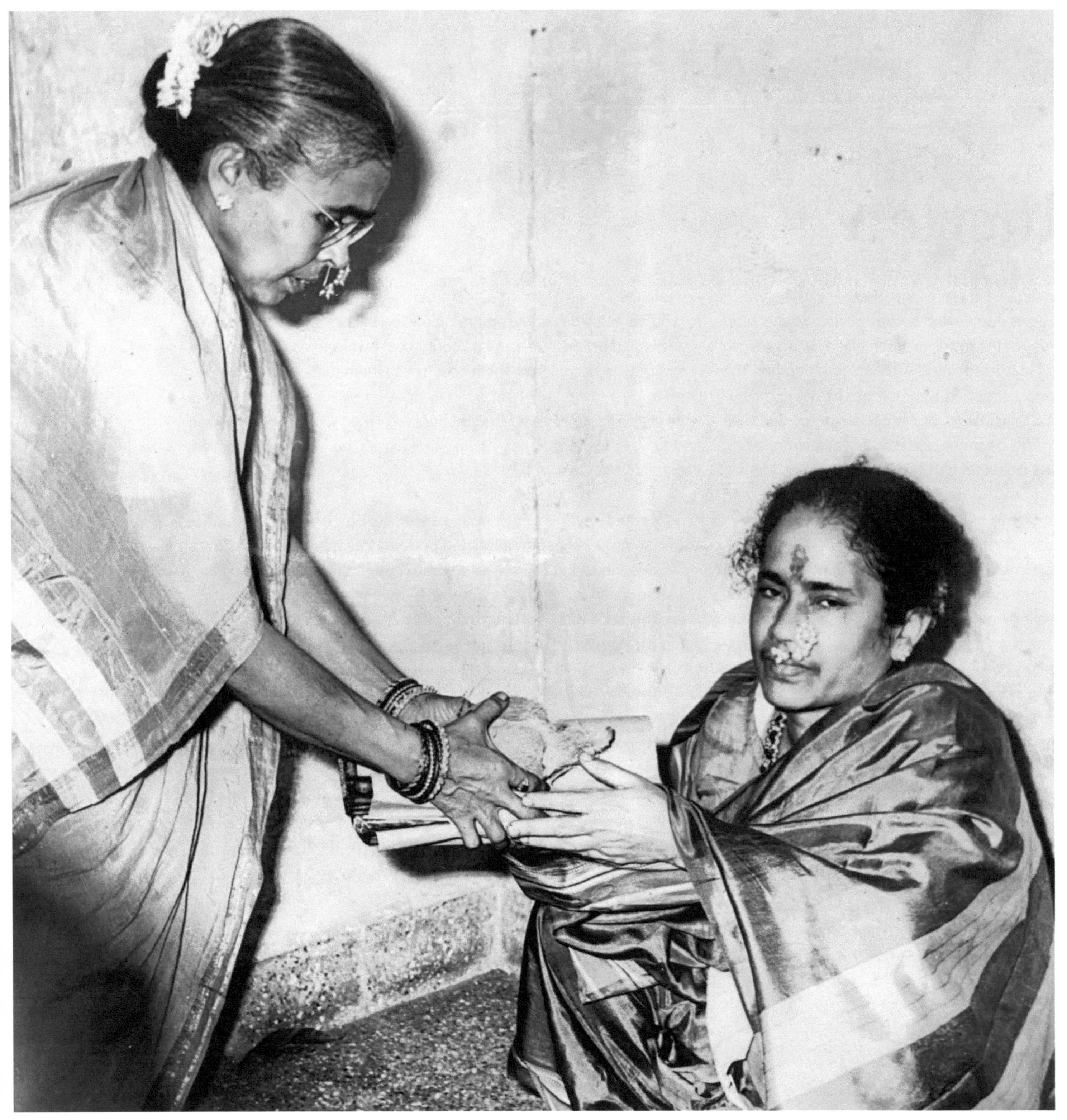

Left : Both my grandmothers at my parents wedding, in December 1969
Top : My mother doing embroidery on a saree, in January 2022

One day, in an emotional mood, I was remembering my grandma. Almost unconsciously, I opened my wardrobe to bring out that saree of hers which I still have as my keepsake. As I felt the soft folds and went down the memory lane of childhood times, my attention was caught by the peculiar weave and texture of the fabric. I began to wonder how it must be made. Intrigued, I did some research, and found a lot of information about the fabric and saree, its name, its origins, where it is made, and also how it compares to other similar types. I was surprised at the amount of information there was to know about this saree, that so far, I only knew as my grandma's green saree. Something was triggered in me, and I began to research about other sarees of my grandma and mom that were always my favorites. This exercise awakened me not just to the vastness of the topic of sarees but also to the immensity of my admiration for this beautiful garment, most of which I owe to my grandma. In that defining moment, I decided to embark upon an endeavor to explore the world of this six yards of fabric, that is innately a part of me. That decision led me into a most pleasurable journey of discovery and appreciation.

Taking inspiration from my Grandma's attitude of being a lifelong student, I began to write notes of my research, and then began documenting them in blogs. I began to share these blogs with close friends, also saree-lovers like me. Encouraged by their response, I began publishing my blogs. One thing led to another, inspiring me to think of compiling these articles into a book. Again, I got immense encouragement, support and active help from several friends and family members. With all of that, this dream has come to fruition.

Sarees are a topic of love for many. To me, they are way more than mere garments - they trigger memories of events and of people, they evoke emotions. They are an integral part not just of my physical memory, but also my emotional memory. Compiling this book allowed me to relive many beautiful memories, dust off many interesting stories from bygone lanes of life. My attempt in this book is to give a voice to these memories, share these stories, and while doing so, also share what I discovered about these sarees, their distinctive features and their interesting history.

Each of the types of sarees portrayed in this book has a personal story to it, a fond memory that ties it to my heart. A saree needs to be perceived not just with sight, touch and feel, but also with the emotions it triggers. My hope is that this book will help you feel and admire these sarees in your mind's eye, often triggering a memory of your own that takes you down your own memory lane. If this book gives you that joy, I would have achieved my objective. And if, along the way, you start noticing features in sarees and recognizing their types, that would be an added bonus.

So, welcome to my world of sarees – stories in six yards!

Kalika Kekkar

KARNATAKA

DHARWAD KASUTI

Simple symmetry

The first saree in this book has to be the one that is most connected with my memories of Grandma, who put me on this journey of exploration; it is also the softest and most worn saree in my wardrobe - the Kasuti saree.

My story about this saree goes back to when I was a young girl, maybe nine or ten years old. It was a Sunday in the month of *Shraavan*, known aptly as a month of festivals. In the month of Shraavan, which falls roughly across July or August per the Julian calendar, almost every day of the week is culturally significant and is enthusiastically celebrated. On this particular Sunday morning, Grandma asked me to get ready for *pooja* (prayers). She patiently answered my multiple questions to explain to me the importance of the Sun, and guided me through the ritual of *Aditya-pooja* (literally translated as "Sun-worship"). After that, in the month of *Shraavan* on every Sunday, I was given the entire responsibility to perform this *pooja* while she sat beside me.

This was not like other traditional *pooja* - this did not involve any idols of Gods or Goddesses. Here, we picked different leaves (at least five varieties) and worshiped them. My job was to go into Grandma's garden, identify and collect the leaves, and arrange them on the *pooja* dias for the ritual. I would fold two of the leaves into a conical shape, their stems gently tucked inside, and place them as idols for the *pooja*, while the other leaves I had collected would go in even layers on top of these two leaf-cones. I loved using some creativity to arrange them differently every time, in symmetrically formed designs. We would then worship these and Grandma would cook leafy vegetables as the special dish of the day, instead of the normal sweets cooked in other such *pooja*. On the last Sunday of the month, she would also cook a sweet (*prasaad*) along with the vegetables, and then we would go to the nearby Babulnath temple (a well-known ancient temple in Mumbai) to offer that *prasaad* to Lord Shiva.

This simple ritual on those four or five Sundays in that month instilled a very important lesson in my young mind - that Nature is God and we need to respect it. I would look forward to every Sunday in the month, and especially to my trip to the temple with Grandma. For this ritual, she would often wear her favorite green Kasuti silk saree. That experience of visiting this lovely temple holding Grandma's hand, the soft touch of Kasuti silk against my skin and its gentle rustle in my ears is a lasting memory in my mind. That image still flashes to my mind whenever I see a Kasuti saree.

Kasuti was the saree type that put me on this fascinating journey of exploring sarees, and I look forward to passing on both - this saree and hopefully this fascination - to my daughter and maybe my grand-daughter someday, like Grandma did to me!

features

Kasuti sarees hail from Dharwad, a small city located to the northwest of Bangalore in the province of Karnataka. The handwoven embroidery on these sarees is a traditional form that can trace its roots to the seventh century AD. Dharwad is famous for sarees in general, and the Kasuti is one of the pallbearers of this fame. The name *Kasuti* comes from the local Kannada language, and means handwork of cotton thread (*Kai* means hand, *Suti* means made of cotton). This embroidery is also commonly known as Karnataki *Kashida*.

Kasuti embroidery consists of interwoven geometric patterns arranged in an interesting design. Patterns are largely adopted from temple designs and architectural patterns in this area. Commonly depicted motifs include elephants, *diya* (lamp), *ratha* (chariot), *chakras* (wheels), stars, *gopura* (temple top) and palanquins. The basic stitch used in this type of embroidery is very simple, called *dhaav-dora* (literal meaning - running thread) in Marathi. However, the stitch is put so carefully and skilfully that patterns are formed on both sides of the fabric, worthy of display on either side. When you see a Kasuti saree, reverse the cloth, and you will notice the same embroidery design on the inside.

Variety is created by building on this simple stitch; some of the stitches employed are *Ganti, Murgi, Neyge* and *Menthe*. *Ganti* is a double running stitch used for marking vertical, horizontal and diagonal lines, *Murgi* is a zig-zag stitch, *Neyge* is a running stitch and *Menthe* is a cross-stitch resembling fenugreek seeds.

The stitch is put so carefully and skilfully that patterns are formed on both sides of the fabric, worthy of display on either side.

GUJARAT

BANDHANI

Colorful knots

A mother's touch is the most soothing. I was sorely longing for my mother's one day, but she was not with me. Time zones did not make it possible to speak to her at the time either. I went to the next best alternative possible - I opened the cupboard which is now full of many of my mother's sarees that she has passed on to me. I picked a couple and sat with them, feeling her warmth seeping through them, calming me down. After some time, I glanced at the sarees, and was surprised to find that both of them, which I had picked at random, were of the same type. I wondered about the odds of that, and took a closer look at the stack, only to realize that this was not a chance event. My mother's wardrobe did have a disproportionate share of this type, as it is one of her favorites - the unmistakably colorful Bandhani.

My mom wore her Bandhani sarees often when I was a kid, their tie-dye work making it easy to identify this saree even for the ten-year-old girl I was back then. They were simple, elegant, and vibrant. I was fascinated by the constellation-like patterns on them. The more I looked at them, the more colorful and numerous the dot patterns seemed. When accompanying my mother on some of her saree-buying trips, I discovered that unlike other sarees, when you buy a traditional authentic Bandhani saree, it comes as a crinkled piece of fabric, with hundreds of threads tied in different places, hardly looking like a saree. I realized that these knots created and hid the beautiful patterns I adored, and when we untied the knots, and stretched and pressed the saree, there unfurled that magical world of dots, circles and squares, beautiful patterns that captured my imagination!

I still remember how my mom had explained the technique and uniqueness of this saree. The name Bandhani comes from the Sanskrit word "*bandha*" meaning a tie or bond; the colloquial name is Bandhej. It is one of the oldest Indian arts still in practice, a technique of tie-dye that works with natural colors to form small circular, dot patterns through a fine and intricate tying process. Since the process involves strategically tying and dyeing the fabric, the crafted products are 100% handmade.

Strangely, despite this early orientation into Bandhani, I didn't own one until very recently. It was probably because of my preference for silk, while Bandhanis come in cottons or georgettes. It was my mom who took me to a shop, where, sitting on the white soft sit-down mattresses, I was awestruck by the sheer varieties of Bandhani sarees in myriad different designs and fabrics. The shop had any color combination I could desire and in any material Bandhani ever touched, from traditional Bandhej to its many variations such as Gharchola, Leheriya, Jaal Upada, Banarasi Bandhani & many more. I would highly recommend anyone interested in Bandhani to definitely visit this place - the Khatri Jamnadas Bechardas shop in Bhuleshwar, Mumbai. I bought my first Bandhani there with my mom, and like her, have not stopped since.

features

The vibrant, lively and colorful Bandhani sarees are available in a myriad designs, bright colors and a variety of fabrics. The best Bandhani work is done in the Indian states of Gujarat and Rajasthan. Since Bandhani is a labor-intensive process involving tying and often multiple rounds of dyeing, it needs resilient fabrics that can withstand the push and pull they are subjected to. That is why Bandhani was initially done only on fabrics and blends of cotton. Over the years, however, the repertoire of fabrics has broadened to make way for contemporary styles and materials. Bandhani sarees are now made in fine cotton, georgette, cotton-silk blends, crepe, chiffon and resilient silk variants such as Gaji silk. Gaji silk base material is thicker, lustrous and smooth, can be dyed in bright colors and is strong enough to withstand heavy embellishments like *zardozi* embroidery.

The art of Bandhani is as exciting as its history. The fabric to be dyed is tied very tightly at different points in knots with thick, impermeable cotton strings and then dyed with colors. During the dyeing process, the part of the cloth covered in thread is protected from the color being used, allowing it to retain its existing color. After every cycle of tying and dyeing, the cloth is left to dry in open air, after which further round(s) of tying-dyeing follow, depending on the pattern. Bandhani needs fine motor skills to skillfully and minutely manipulate the fabric for tying, just as it needs extensive knowledge of color schemes and expertise in dyeing materials.

The basic shades of Bandhani print are red, yellow, green, and blue. Each of these is symbolic, for instance, red stands for married life and green for fertility. The common dot pattern designs are, *boond* (a small dot with a dark center), *laddu-jalebi* (circles and spirals in pattern), *dungar shahi* (mountain pattern), *kodi* (tear or drop pattern), & *tikunthi* (pattern of circles and squares in a group of three). Traditional patterns include *leheriya, mothra, ekdali* and *shikari* depending on the manner in which the cloth has been tied. An intricate design in a saree would have approximately 75,000 dots.

The common dot pattern designs are, boond (a small dot with a dark center), laddu-jalebi (circles and spirals in pattern), dungar shahi (mountain pattern), kodi (tear or drop pattern), & tikunthi (pattern of circles and squares in a group of three).

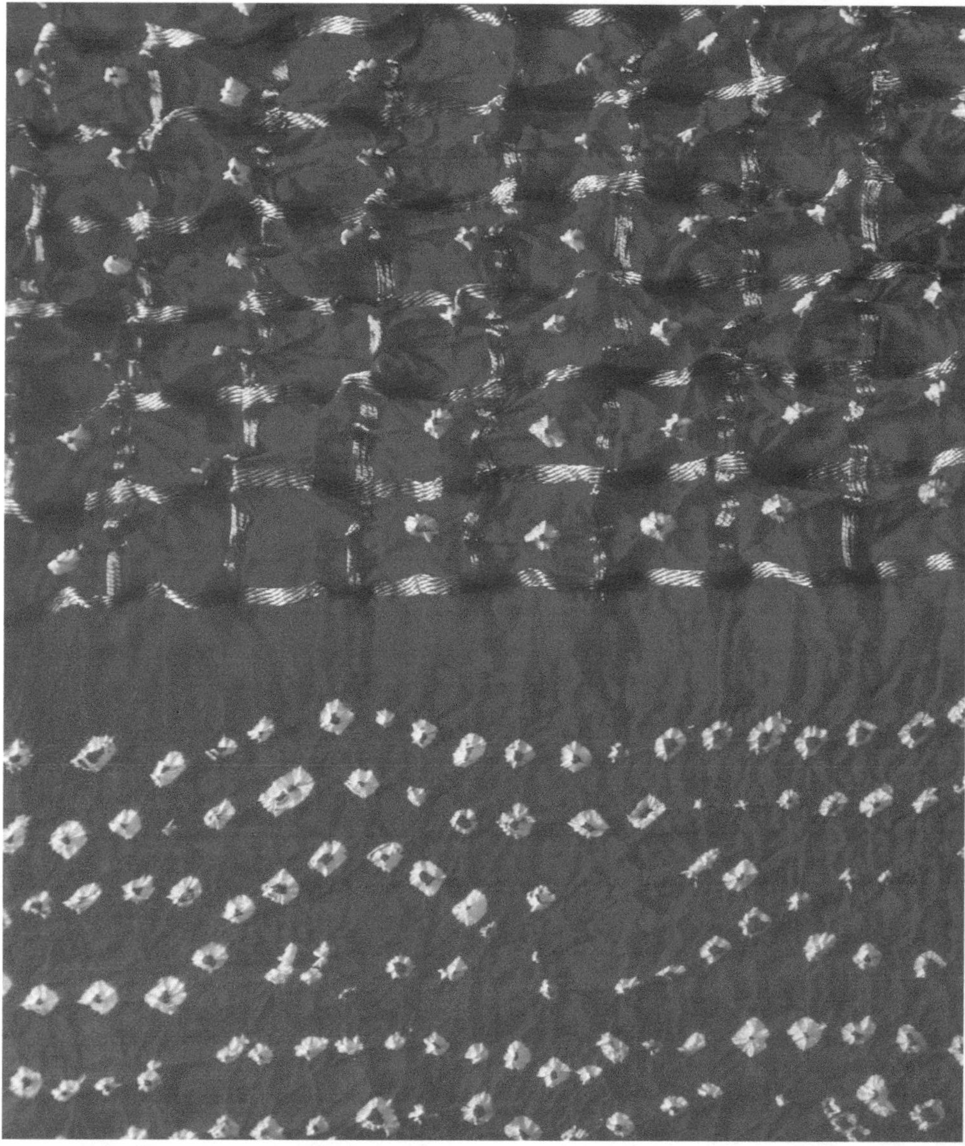

Gharchola: Each traditional Gharchola saree is a variant of the popular Bandhani saree. Gharchola is distinguishable by its typical grid pattern, with each single square flaunting a Bandhani design in it, achieved by tying the base in a certain way. Once embellished with Bandhani patterns, Gharchola is further lovingly decorated with intricate embroidery.

BANGLADESH & WEST BENGAL

JAMDANI

Vase of flowers

"For we women are not only the deities of the household fire, but the flame of the soul itself." — Rabindranath Tagore, The Home and the World.

Gurudev Rabindranath Tagore, a towering figure in recent Indian history, was a multi-talented personality. His contributions to literature as a writer, poet, singer and lyricist in his native Bengali, as well as in English, are invaluable. What is lesser known, however, is his and his family's contribution to the world of fashion. The Tagore family was well-known for being a style-conscious household. His father was actively involved in styling the way the girls in his family dressed. The common way in which a saree is worn in India today with the pleated *pallu* pinned to the left shoulder and with a paired blouse and petticoat was an innovation brought in by Tagore's trailblazing sister-in-law, Jnanadanandini Devi. Being surrounded by such a fashion-conscious family imbibed an importance for attire in Rabindranath too. He considered one's dress to be a facet of individuality. He applied the same to his characters and was therefore explicit about how individual characters in his stories dressed.

I was always intrigued by Tagore's soft yet strong, independent-minded women protagonist characters portrayed in his various novels and poems such as "Banshi". Characters like Binodini from Chokher Bali (Speck in the Eye), the iconic Charulata from Nastanirh (The Broken Nest), Mrinmoyee from Samapti (The Conclusion), Mrinal from Strir Patra (A Wife's Letter) and Suman from Tyaga (The Renunciation), all strong women, have left a profound mark on my mind. No wonder Tagore chose the Jamdani saree for his leading ladies, not just making them look lovelier, but adding a distinctive signature trait to their strong personalities. When I think of these characters, I cannot but help thinking of the Jamdani - like these characters, it stands for distinctive identity, dignity and self-recognition.

The Jamdani saree is a gorgeous weave that stands out for its class & beauty. The word Jamdani has a Persian origin, and literally means a vase of flowers ("*Jam*" means flower, "*Dani*" means a vase or a container). The name indicates the specialty of these sarees - beautiful floral motifs woven in patterns. Some Jamdani sarees also feature geometric patterns or figures in place of flowers. Whether with figures or flowers, the Jamdani design is poetry woven in cotton, so beautiful that it would stand out even in the midst of silk weaves.

I always give my mother a bouquet of flowers for Mother's Day. Having been awakened to the beauty of the Jamdani, I gifted her with a different bouquet this time - an exquisite Dhakai Jamdani. For good measure, I also indulged myself with a similar gift - an elegant Tangail Jamdani. A very popular choice of women, I am sure the Jamdani will be adored and worn by generations of ladies to come.

features

The Jamdani is made from a highly breathable sheer cotton fabric, vividly patterned and traditionally woven on a handloom. This art has been in practice around the city of Dhaka in Bangladesh for over five hundred years. The term *Dhakai* Jamdani or simply *Dhakai* saree is often used to denote any Jamdani saree. Jamdani sarees, with their unparalleled softness, beauty and heritage, are an essential part of every Bengali woman's wardrobe.

The final look it achieves is of vibrant patterns appearing to float on the surface of a fine, transparent fabric.

Indian Jamdani sarees are made mostly in West Bengal but also in other parts of the country. They are classified based on the type of motifs they feature or the region where they are produced. Regional variations include *Tangail* Jamdani, *Shantipur* Jamdani, *Dhaniakhali* Jamdani and as *Uppada* in Andhra Pradesh.

A remarkable trait of this weaving technique is that the pattern is not sketched or outlined on the fabric. Instead, it is drawn on graph paper and placed underneath the warp. During the weaving process, the pattern beneath the warp threads acts as a trace to set up the design onto the saree. Weaving these sarees needs two weavers, and the designs are worked in link embroidery through a special technique called the supplemental weft technique. It is a laborious and time-consuming process. But it is well worth the effort because the final look it achieves is of vibrant patterns appearing to float on the surface of a fine, transparent fabric - a marked feature of Jamdani weaves.

The weaving techniques differ for some types of Jamdanis. For instance, the embroidery thread is inserted after every ground pick in a *Dhakai* Jamdani but after every two ground picks in *Tangails*, giving different looks. The main characteristic of *Tangails* is the extra weft *buttis*, which are tiny motifs repeated all over the fabric.

KARNATAKA

ILKAL

Harmony in contrast

India is rich with many different cultures in its microcosm of diversity. Languages are a big part of these cultures. While Mumbai, the city I was born and brought up in, is very cosmopolitan there are some parts of the city where the Marathi influence is unmistakable.

Dadar, a central suburb of Mumbai soaked in quintessential Marathi culture, is associated with many childhood memories appealing to my Marathi roots. Dadasaheb Phalke Road proudly flaunts the name of the nation's first movie maker, while the large and arterial Tilak bridge commemorates a prominent national hero, both hailing from Marathi families. Ranade Road features fruit and vegetable vendors selling fresh produce from near-by villages, jewelry and saree shops, many selling traditional Marathi designs, and Dadar Flower Market brims with flowers of every hue and fragrance, fit for every occasion. Both are abuzz with activity at any and all times. Even today, the fragrance of *mogra gajras* (small jasmine garlands worn by women in their hair) takes my mind back to the environs of Dadar.

One of the oldest saree shops here is Girgaon Panche Depot, a small fabric shop on N.C. Kelkar Road - a shop we visited very often (like every Marathi family would) to purchase a nine-yard (*nau-vaari*) saree or a *khunn* (a special bordered fabric for a saree-blouse) for religious ceremonies. This shop was my mother's first choice to buy Ilkal sarees - the very traditional Marathi sarees that were a mainstay of all the old Marathi movies and plays I saw in Plaza and Shivaji Mandir. While old black-and-white movies only gave me a greyscale impression of these, my frequent visits to Girgaon Panche Depot had familiarized me to the colorful world of these sarees - their beautiful maroon borders, the burst of red in their *pallus* and the striking contrast of colors in their checkered or plain striped bodies. As I understood this, I also began to notice that most of the Ranade Road green grocer and flower grocer women wore these Ilkal cotton sarees matched with *khunn* satin brocade blouses, just like the women characters I had seen in period dramas, showing how alive this tradition was even in modern times.

This saree is called Irkal in Marathi, though its original name is Ilkal, the name of a small town in Karnataka. The most defining feature of an Ilkal saree is its bright red traditional woven border and a matching bright red *pallu*, probably inspired by and depicting the bright ruby-red granite mined in Ilkal. These sarees, woven in both cotton and silk, are simple in design, without any intricate patterns. Their beauty is defined by the elegance they exude in their simplicity and in the harmony they show in contrasting colors. I have worn handwoven lightweight Ilkal sarees in pure silk many times; they always stand out gracefully even in a crowd of heavier ones. I believe that this saree with its simple design elements symbolizes how harmony can be achieved even with bold, contrasting differences to create a beautiful, harmonious design.

features

Ilkal sarees are widely and commonly used in the interiors of Maharashtra, north Karnataka and Andhra Pradesh. Ilkal is a small town, located in the South-East part of the Bagalkot district in Karnataka. Ilkal was an ancient weaving center where weaving seems to have started in the 8th century AD. The growth of this industry and hence this saree is attributed to the patronage provided by the local chieftains in and around the town of Bellary. Due to its unique placement in central Karnataka, it also crossed borders into the states of Maharashtra and Andhra Pradesh, gaining popularity there.

A unique and distinguishing characteristic of the saree is a weaving technique used exclusively in Ilkal, wherein the body warp is joined with the *pallu* warp, locally known as *Tope Teni*. The main body of the saree may be plain or may carry designs such as stripes, rectangles, squares. The *pallu* of the Ilkal saree carries designs of temple towers. The *pallu* is usually made of red silk with white patterns. Normally in *Tope Teni seragu pallu*, three solid portions would be in red color, and in between two portions in white color. The beauty of *Tope Teni seragu* is further enhanced at times by weaving in its middle portion, yet another design known as *Kyadgi*.

The saree is either made of cotton, silk, or a mixture of the two. The colors are mostly earthy yet vibrant, such as pomegranate red, peacock green, indigo, mustard and parrot green. The body of the saree is of a dark or bright color, plain or with small checks (called *tirki*) running across its length. A highlight of this saree is its border, 2.5 to 4 inches wide, usually using vividly contrasting colors. These traditional borders are of different types, such as (a) *gomi* (more popularly known as Ilkal *dadi*), (b) *paraspet* (Sub-divided into *chikki paras* and *dodd paras*), (c) *gaadi*, (d) *jari* or (e) contemporary *gayathri*.

A unique and distinguishing characteristic of the saree is a weaving technique used exclusively in Ilkal, wherein the body warp is joined with the pallu warp, locally known as Tope Teni.

In Maharashtra, blouses made of *khunn*, which is a satin brocade fabric, are commonly paired with Ilkal saree. While Ilkal is relatively unknown outside of the 3 states mentioned above, in recent years, this fabric has got a new fresh resurgence as modern designers have begun using Ilkal in fashion shows, and Ilkal blouses are seen more and more being used to match with different sarees - testimony to the beauty and uniqueness of the design and pattern of these sarees, which have stood the test of time.

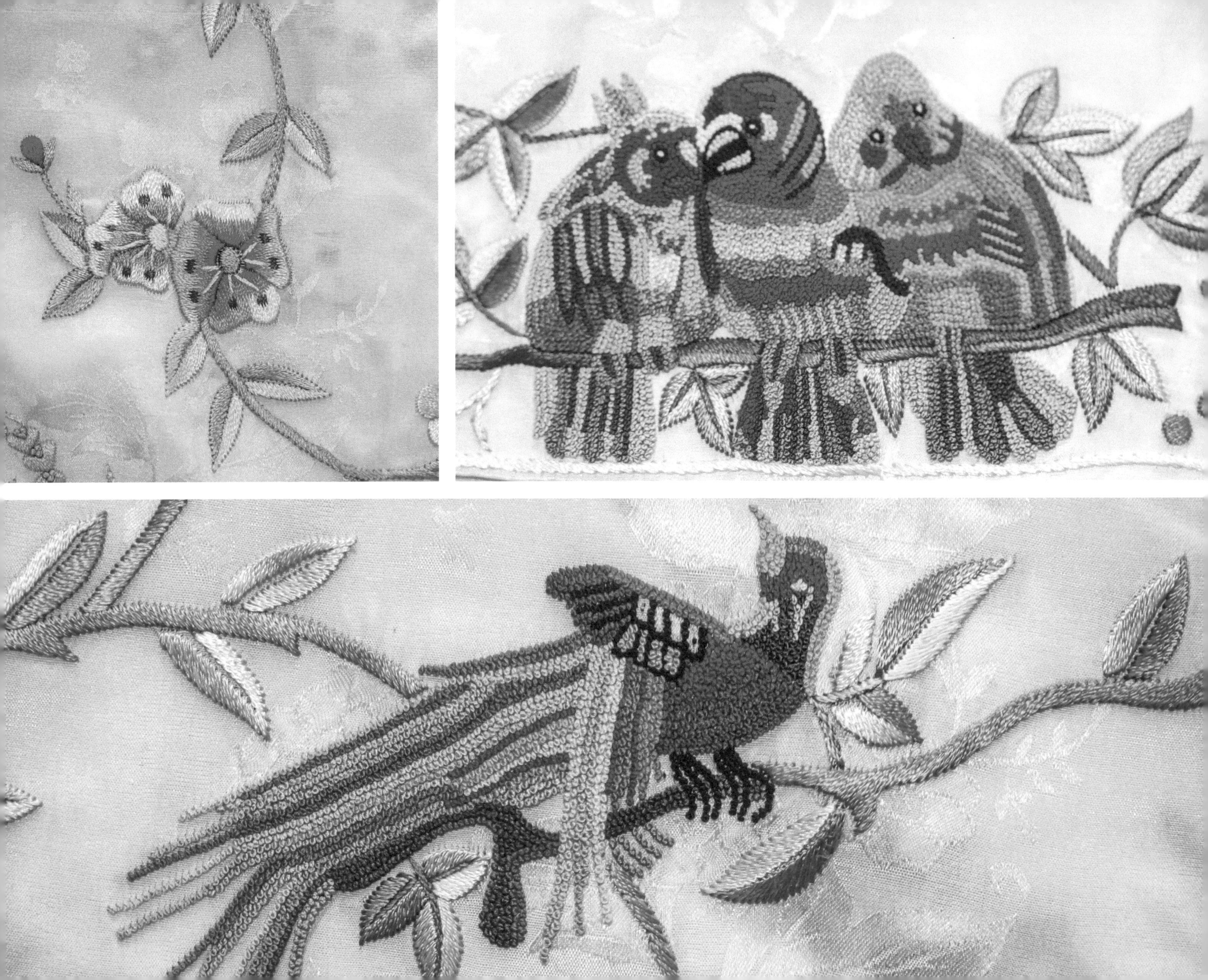

GUJARAT & MUMBAI

GARA

Style in tradition

Women wear sarees with love and pride. I remember Ms. Indra Nooyi (former CEO of PepsiCo) mentioning in her famously Rashtrapati Bhavan visit, how she chooses to wear Kanjivarams for power dressing. Many women share this sentiment -- often reflecting on how wearing a saree makes them feel authentic, rooted, and empowered. While Indra Nooyi brought the saree to the American C-suite board rooms, decades earlier, the ex- Prime Minister of India, Mrs Indira Gandhi brought the saree onto the global stage. She wore a saree to almost all her public appearances, and her eclectic choice of sarees remained a part of her signature powerful persona.

Mrs. Gandhi always wore simple yet elegant handloom sarees that were exclusively woven by craftsmen across India. That's why a picture of her wearing an atypically bright red festive saree published in the newspaper one day caught my attention. The picture was taken at a private family event that she had attended. She looked stylish yet traditional in the exquisite red saree she wore, which was embroidered all over in golden silk thread. She had paired the saree with a matching sleeveless blouse. The caption described the saree as a Gara saree; that's how I was introduced to the lovely Gara, with the image of Mrs. Gandhi wearing one imprinted on my mind.

Gara sarees are typical of Parsi women, and are worn mostly in traditional Parsi functions. Zoroastrians or Parsis are a small closely-knit community in India (Mrs. Gandhi was married into this community). Attending Parsi functions is a privilege of the experience of living in Mumbai. Mostly weddings or *Navjote's* (initiation ceremonies), these functions are traditional affairs celebrated in fire temples called *Agiyari* (worship place) that are located close to Parsi colonies called *baug*. Gara sarees, that are fondly treasured as priceless heirlooms passed from mother to daughter, and are taken out of treasure chests at traditional functions. Unlike the Kanjivaram and Banarasi sarees that are woven, the Gara is laboriously hand-embroidered. Gara embroidery is intricate, combining elegance and aesthetics. Parsi women drape the saree slightly differently, making it different and distinctive from the usual saree drape. Customized to this style of draping, the corner of the *pallu* or *pallav* of a Gara saree is left unembroidered as this bit is tucked in at the waist when worn in this unique style.

The Parsi Gara is thus a unique combination of tradition, style and elegance - delicately embellished, aesthetically colorful, glamorously stylish yet authentically ethnic.

features

The word "*gara*" (also *ghara*) is said to stem from the Gujarati word for a saree. The Gara is an excellent example of how artistic trends and techniques traveled across the world. It was fascinating for me to learn that the Sassanian "Circlet of Pearls" motif traveled all the way from Zoroastrian Persia to China during the Tang Dynasty and then found its way back to India in the Parsi embroidered gara ("*gaaj*" or "*paaj*" or "*gaji*"). This unique technique of embroidery tradition has its roots in Iran and drew on influences from European, Chinese, Persian and Indian cultures. Persian or Farsi (Parsi) traders who also visited China in those times, brought this to India.

The *pallav* or *pallu* is the portion or panel of the saree that drapes over the shoulder and chest, while the part that goes over the head is called a *saur*. The amount of embroidery in the body of a Gara can vary - it could be relatively plain with small motifs sprinkled on it, or heavy with a dense all-over *jaal* pattern. As far as the border goes, it could be an elaborate one that's part of the main body, or it could be a separate border (plain or embroidered) that is stitched onto the saree. Whatever the body and the border type, the *pallu* is always heavily embroidered. In terms of colors, a typical Gara body may be dark with ivory threadwork or pastel-shaded with multi-colored threadwork, in which there could be as many as thirty shades. While the Satin stitch is largely used in Parsi embroidery, many other types such as the Crewel stitch, Stem stitch, *Khaka* stitch and French knot. Whatever the type, this thread work is always intricate and fine. Legend goes that the *Khaka* stitch is so fine that it would cause the artisans to have failing eyesight, giving it the name "the forbidden stitch".

Typically seen motifs in Gara sarees are inspired by nature, using patterns of flowers (lotus, peonies, roses, lilies, leaves), trees (weeping willow, cherry, pine, maple, bamboo) and birds (phoenix, cranes, peacocks, swans, parrots).

Each motif is symbolic, for instance, lilies stand for health, chrysanthemums for long life, the hundred-petal rose for spiritualism, divine fungus for longevity and immortality, and the swaying cypress tree for life and eternity.

The Persian symbol of *chakla-chakli* (male-female sparrow) is a unique, much-loved motif used in Gara embroidery. Each motif is symbolic, for instance, lilies stand for health, chrysanthemums for long life, the hundred-petal rose for spiritualism, divine fungus for longevity and immortality, and the swaying cypress tree for life and eternity. Along with these natural elements, motifs also feature Chinese cultural elements like pagodas, boats, traditional building structures & human figures depicted in fine, delicate embroidery.

WEST BENGAL

BALUCHARI

Silken tales

The beauty of a saree, which is only a long piece of cloth, comes out in the way it is draped around the body. There are many different ways in which a saree is draped, typically varying by region and community. Among all the drapes, I have great fascination for the Bengali drape style. Whenever I think of this drape, my mind's eye sees a huge nineteenth-century *zamindar haveli* (mansion of a rich land-owner) in Bengal, an enigmatic Suchitra Sen (famous Bengali actor) standing in the doorway, her beauty enhanced by a big round red bindi on the forehead, her gorgeous jewelry, her beautiful dark hair loosely hanging on her back and a gorgeous saree with the loosely hanging *pallu* casually yet deliberately tossed over the left shoulder and held in place by a heavy bunch of keys. This image from the televised portrayal of Sarat Chandra Chattopadhyay's stories, permanently etched in my mind, was my initiation into the world of Bengali *zamindars* and that of the Bengali style saree drape. I was as mesmerized by the power and aristocracy of these *Zamindar* women characters brought alive by Sen's acting prowess as by the portrayal of their wealth, brought out by the sarees chosen for her costumes, many of them being openly opulent Balucharis.

Of the wide variety of sarees that Bengal is home to, the Jamdani, Baluchari and Tant are the most popular. While Jamdani and Tant sarees are typically in cotton, the Baluchari saree is usually woven in silk. The Baluchari's *pallu* end-piece, adorned with designs widely ranging from the simple to the sensational, is its most distinguishing feature. The Baluchari *pallu* is known to have a huge variety of motifs, including unusual ones like the figurines of the terracotta temples of Barangore. Baluchari sarees, intricately woven with unique craftsmanship, ooze grandeur from every thread.

Little wonder that a Bengali woman's treasured collection of traditional sarees is sure to include at least one Baluchari. To me, the Baluchari and Suchitra Sen both will always be symbolic of the bewitching beauty of Bengal.

features

The origin of the Baluchari weaving tradition dates back to the early eighteenth century, and stems from a small village named Baluchar, on the banks of river Bhagirathi in West Bengal. The original Baluchari sarees in the eighteenth and nineteenth centuries were woven with silk thread on silk fabric on traditional *jaala* (pit) looms. During the revival of Baluchari weaving in the 20th century by weavers in Bishnupur, the *jaala* was replaced by the jacquard technique of weaving. Although this technique has reduced the time taken for weaving a Baluchari saree significantly, the saree motifs are no longer reversible, as they were with the original method.

> *Baluchari sarees have very elaborate pallus and borders, often depicting complete scenes or stories.*

Baluchari sarees have very elaborate *pallus* and borders, often depicting complete scenes or stories. These stories could be from mythological texts like the Ramayana and Mahabharata, or from lives of Nawabs of Bengal; they could be reproductions of terracotta decorations that adorned old temples, including images of beautiful women in interesting postures like when riding a horse, smelling a flower or even smoking a hookah. The motif of *Kalka* (a curved raw mango pattern, resembling large paisley or a stylized leaf) is used extensively in the intricate designs.

Baluchari sarees are broadly categorized based on the colors of threads used in weaving. Baluchar *bootidars* (embroiders) avoid strong contrast - they choose minimal colors which don't contrast with or stand out from each other, but rather merge into each other and harmonize with its background. Simple Baluchari sarees have the entire pattern woven in a single color of *resham* (silk) threads. The more colorful Baluch""aris - Meenakaari Baluchari sarees - have threads in two or more colors with attractive *meenakaari* work that brightens the patterns. The grandest Baluchari sarees, known as Swarnachari sarees, are woven with gold or silver colored threads that illuminate the patterns to a beautiful dazzle, often with *meenakaari* work in another color.

TELANGANA

GADWAL

Gossamer grace

"To plant a garden, is to believe in tomorrow."
- Audrey Hepburn

Grandma had a green thumb - her terrace garden was rich and fragrant with several varieties of flowers - *Bela, Chameli, Gulbakshi, Mogra & Sontakka* (local names) would spread their perfume in the terrace and the entire house. The garden produced enough flowers for Grandpa to make garlands for his morning *pooja* (prayers).

The garden was a site of many beautiful afternoons, when Grandma would regale me with stories after tea. We would wait together to see *Gulbakshi* (Mirabilis Jalapa) flower buds open up at their normal late time in the day. She would then carefully pluck these flowers. While Grandpa made garlands for the daily *pooja*, Grandma would make them for special occasions like festivals or special *pooja*. Unlike Grandpa's garlands which were made by tying flowers together with a thread, Grandma's garlands, often made of *Gulbakshi* flowers, were made without threads, just by weaving flowers into each other, something I always found intriguing. I would eagerly wait to see Grandma's sarees on such occasions - typically she wore a certain type of cotton sarees for these events, with a fine self-checkered pattern all over. Grandma's petite figure clad in those beautiful sarees and her tender beautiful smile that lit up the entire household will always be one of my warmest childhood memories. Little wonder then that *Gulbakshi* flowers trigger for me the memory of her smile and her sarees, which I now know were Gadwal sarees.

Gadwal sarees are woven in silk and cotton alike. The silk ones are known for their beautiful *zari* work and well-crafted *kuttu* borders, while the cotton varieties also flaunt a rich and subtle look. These sarees are known for a unique combination of a classy and traditional look, while also being easy to wear and handle. The other unique feature of these sarees is the range of colors they offer, the beautiful color combinations between the body and the border/*pallu*, and the exquisite shades they flaunt, with traditional colors made softer with earthy tones. Cotton Gadwal sarees are woven all over with a small checkered pattern on the main base, with woven *zari* border in a contrasting color. The *pallu* of a Gadwal is woven in the same color as that of its border, and may have heavy brocade.

The colorful combinations offered by Gadwal sarees often take me back to my childhood and to memories of the garlands my Grandma made of different colors of the *Gulbakshi* flowers in her garden. To me, Gadwal sarees are just like *Gulbakshi* flowers, delicate, charming and full of possibilities of combining colors like only they can.

features

Gadwal Sarees get their name from their home - Gadwal town in Telangana state, situated between the Krishna and Tungabhadra Rivers. Most Gadwal sarees are woven with interlocked weft borders (called *Tippadamu* locally in Telugu) of contrasting colors. While brocade embroidery skills of Gadwal weavers are said to trace back to Varanasi, the designs show no resemblance with those of the Banarasi style; on the contrary, they are strongly and authentically south-east Indian in structure and aesthetic quality.

A checkered self-design in the body is a unique quality of a traditional Gadwal cotton saree.

The popular variety of Gadwal sarees are the ones in cotton base with borders in pure Mulberry or Tussar silk. A checkered self-design in the body is a unique quality of a traditional Gadwal cotton saree. A pure silk Gadwal saree is magnificent yet delicate, usually woven in bright contrasting colors. Resplendent Gadwal silk sarees are woven with longer, heavily brocaded *pallus* with golden *zari* and *buttis* or checks all over the body. The large *zari* border with a *kaddi* line (a line running through the length of the border parallel to the edge, completely woven in gold or silver *zari*) and the *pallu* decorated with beautiful motifs like flowers, *rudraksh* (holy beads), paisley, diagonal lines, peacocks, *annapakshis* (swans) and *yaalis* (a powerful mythical beast), add a unique charm to this suave weave.

Gadwal sarees, as mentioned before, are known for their rich color combinations, not just of the broad variety of colors but also multiple shades of the same color. For instance, Gadwal greens appear in a broad palette including jade, fern, emerald, pine, mint, olive; oranges boast of hues of carrot, bronze, tangerine, peach, *aboli*, amber, pumpkin, ochre; purples could range from dark purple, plum, mauve to burgundy or sangria; while yellows range from mango, mustard, banana, tawny brown, cider to apricot. The list can go on. The Gadwal saree, with its many exciting colors and endless possibilities of combinations, is a true tribute to the colors of life.

MAHARASHTRA

PAITHANI

Regal splendor

Paithani - regality and splendor in six yards. The memory of how I was introduced to this saree is as beautiful as the saree itself. It was the exciting time of selecting sarees for my wedding. As an ardent fan of Tussar silk and *resham* (silk) embroidery versus heavy silks and *zari* embroidery, I wanted to wear these lighter sarees for the wedding. My mother and mother-in-law both had a more traditional approach in mind, with heavy *zari* sarees for the bride. They collectively took up the challenge to convince me to wear a heavy *zari* saree. They used different techniques for that - they discussed, debated with me, gently cajoled me, and finally came down to a practical negotiation - two sarees of my choice (one for pre-wedding rituals and one for the main wedding ceremony) if I agreed to a Paithani for the reception. Seeing how it was the joint choice of these two saree experts when negotiating with me, I agreed to explore this type.

Soon we were at the saree shop with the objective to choose the Paithani I would wear. As the salesperson enthusiastically opened up a treasure box of the most exclusive wedding Paithani sarees, my attention went straight to the exquisite vibrant saree pallus which were like beautiful kaleidoscopes of colorful peacocks - some with their plumes folded, others with plumes fanned out, some in gold *zari* and others in color. These designs were mostly on *pallus* but some were on borders and in the body too. These beautiful, colorful birds on lovely silk dazzled only like Paithanis do and left me forever in awe of this stunningly beautiful saree.

Named after the town where they originated, Paithani sarees are said to be poetry hand-woven in gold and silk. A typical Paithani can be identified by some distinguishing characteristics. First and foremost - the front and the back of the saree, including the border and *pallu*, look identical, a result of the tapestry method of weaving, which also gives the saree its regal appearance. The border of a Paithani is another distinguishing feature, with its unique pattern of oblique squares. And then of course, is the gleaming, dazzling gold-and-color *pallu* with its unique motifs of birds and flowers - peacocks, parrots and lotuses in different artistic depictions.

So, it was on that shopping trip that I discovered this splendid gem, and I silently thanked my two mothers for making me select this lovely saree for my important day. Thus started my love affair with the Paithani; from that moment onwards, there was no looking back. New Paithanis kept gracing my wardrobe as I wore them happily on occasions and at family events. By now, both mothers are convinced that they have passed down their love and care for the Paithani to this daughter, to be passed onward some day to their grandaughter.

features

The art of weaving a Paithani is many centuries old, developed in the historic city of Paithan in Aurangabad district, Maharashtra. It was a fabric of choice of the women in the household of the Peshwas of Pune, who patronized this art by getting weavers to settle in Yeola, a small town near Shirdi. Here, the Paithani acquired new dimensions in both design and popularity. *Asavali*, the motif of a flowering vine, is credited to the Peshwa period.

Paithani designs are exceptionally alluring, with grandiose borders and pallus.

Paithani designs are exceptionally alluring, with grandiose borders and *pallus*. Paithani saree weaving is comprehensive; some of its distinctive features include weaving, motifs and colors.

Weaving: A Paithani has three sections - borders, base and *pallu*. The intricate inlay borders are created with an interlocked weft technique. Most hand-woven Paithanies are woven in *Kad/Ekdhoti* technique, with a single weft shuttle, thus mixing base color thread into the border. *Kadiyal* Paithani (called "*Parativ*" in local Marathi) is woven with three individual weft shuttles, one each for the lower and the upper border and one for the base. This allows any color combination for the border and the base, allowing borders in the same or contrast colors with reference to the base. This unique way of weaving also means that both sides of the Paithani look exactly the same, with no threads left hanging.

Motifs: Paithani borders have different motifs - *narali* (coconut), *pankha* (fan shape) and *barwa* (twelve strands of a ladder) are common ones. The traditional saree variety comes with a 28-inch *pallu* design. Brocade Paithani saree, on the other hand, has a decorated *pallu* design of 40 inches, in addition to the border and over-the-shoulder part having elaborate motifs woven on it.

Many different motifs are used on the *pallu* - *munia* brocade (parrots), lotus brocade, & *bangadi mor* (peacock woven in a bangle shape) are common. Other beautiful motifs such as *hans* (swan), *asharfi* or *paisa* (coin), *rui phool* (cotton flower), *panja* (a flower in a geometrical shape), *tara* (star), *chandrakor* (crescent moon) and leaf clusters of three leaves also show up frequently, often also on the main body of the saree.

Hues: The special hues of Paithani silk are another distinguishing feature - sometimes single colors, and sometimes multiple colors that show a myriad shades on the saree, depending on the light falling on it. Paithanis of specific colors have special names, *Chandrakala* (black with red border), *Shirodak* (white), *Pheroze* (a blend of green, white and red), and *Kusumbi* (purplish red) to name a few.

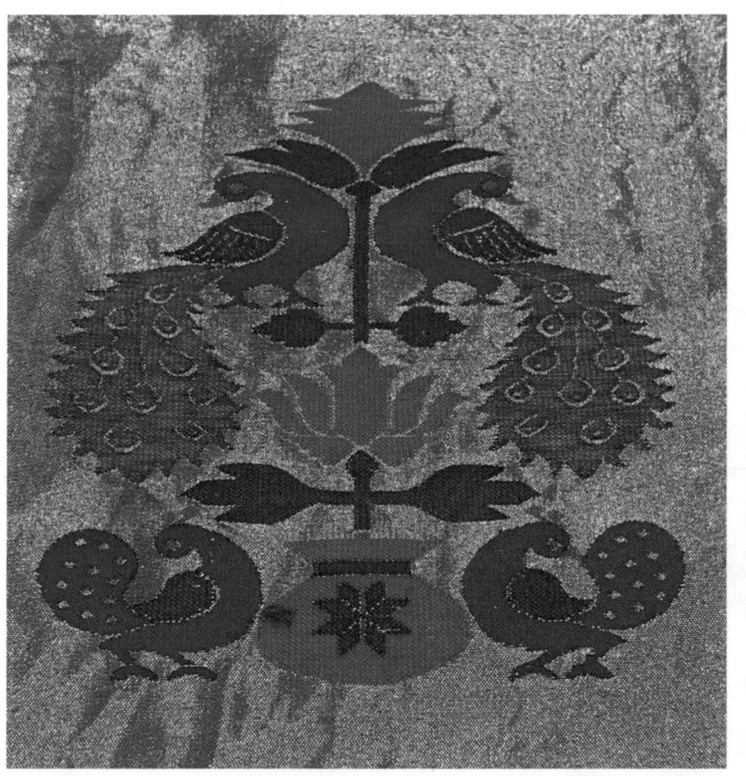

GOA

KUNBI

Rustic charm

Goa - a quintessential holiday destination that to most people, means sun and sand. To me, this province on the western coast of India is much more than that. Summer vacations spent in Goa have given me life-long memories of lovely drives, beautiful sylvan villages, fun-filled beaches of Colva, and yummy food - seasonal fruits like mangoes, jackfruit and cashew fruits, mouthwatering dishes of fish and the soul-satisfying *kokum sol-kadhi* (curry) with rice. But it was only during one monsoon trip to Goa, that I saw the real beauty of this place.

The heavy rains that the state gets in monsoons makes it so verdant that it is at its most beautiful in this season. It was during the rains that we drove from Mapusa in the northern part of Goa to Margao in the south, right through to Karwar in neighboring Karnataka. It was definitely one of the most beautiful road trips I have taken. As we left the cities behind, the landscape outside changed, alternating between clusters of tall coconut trees swaying in the wind and rain, and lush green rice paddy fields soaking in the wetness. And even in that really wet wetness, workers, both men and women, labored in these fields to transplant rice from one part of the field to another (an essential step in the rice-growing process), shin-deep in mud and rainwater, protecting their heads and backs partly with traditional bamboo rain-covers.

These paddy workers are locally called "*Kunbi*"s. They are a tribal community whose traditional occupation is tilling rice fields. I noticed that the women working in the fields alongside men wore their sarees in a way that was very different from any I had seen before; this enabled them to work unhindered in the mud-filled paddy fields. As I was trying to figure out this unusual drape, I noticed the design of the sarees which seemed to be more or less similar among all of them - a distinctive checkered pattern, that I now know is the highlight of this type of saree - the working woman's sturdy Kunbi saree.

To weather the tough conditions in which it is used, the Kunbi saree is made in cotton with a strong and durable weave. Traditionally, it is woven in red and white checks. However, this ancient indigenous fabric of tribal communities has now caught the fancy of new fashion designers, resulting in the Kunbi saree being given a modern touch in the past two decades. With new designs added to the simple aesthetics of this saree, the modern Kunbi saree has now become a mix of the ethnic with the modern, making it a sought-after fabric in modern handloom-lovers' wardrobes.

Goa has a monsoon tradition - the onset of this season is celebrated by people congregating at a special market to buy spices, pickles and dried fish, to be used in the upcoming wet season. This occasion is called *Purumentachem* (*Purument* in Konkani, the local language of Goa, means "provision"). I want to visit this *Purument* market in Margao, Goa at least once in my lifetime, wearing a soft, breathable Kunbi saree - my little tribute to Goa's native Kunbi heritage.

features

Goa used to be a hub for handloom weaving and many weavers had flourishing workshops that produced Kunbi sarees and *kaashti's* (a loin cloth for men). One can't trace the timing of the origins of this saree; it is certainly centuries old. The weave, however, disappeared during Portuguese rule. It wasn't until 1961, that the saree made a modest reappearance.

The Kunbi tribe is believed to be the oldest tribe of Goa. This Kunbi saree was originally worn by *Kunbi* and *Gauda* tribe women who earned their livelihood from working in paddy fields. The Kunbi ladies wore it tied high up to their knees with a knot over the left shoulder and fastened on the back. This allowed them to do their work without the bother of the saree either obstructing their movement in rain and mud, or getting stuck in shrubs and trees when moving around dry fields. This ethnic saree was initially worn without a *choli* (blouse), however at some point in its use, women started to wear it with a simple puffed sleeves blouse.

The traditional Kunbi saree is easily recognizable by its sturdy weave knitted in small and large checks in red and white, and its solid dobby (geometric or floral pattern) border. With its recent popularity, it has got a touch of modern fashion with more colors added to its palette by designers. So, today, one can see yellow, purple, green, blue & black colors in the checkered pattern, adding to the traditional charm. The border thickness ranges from an inch to an inch and a half, and is patterned with close brightly red colored warp threads.

The traditional Kunbi saree is easily recognizable by its sturdy weave knitted in small and large checks in red and white, and its solid dobby (geometric or floral pattern) border.

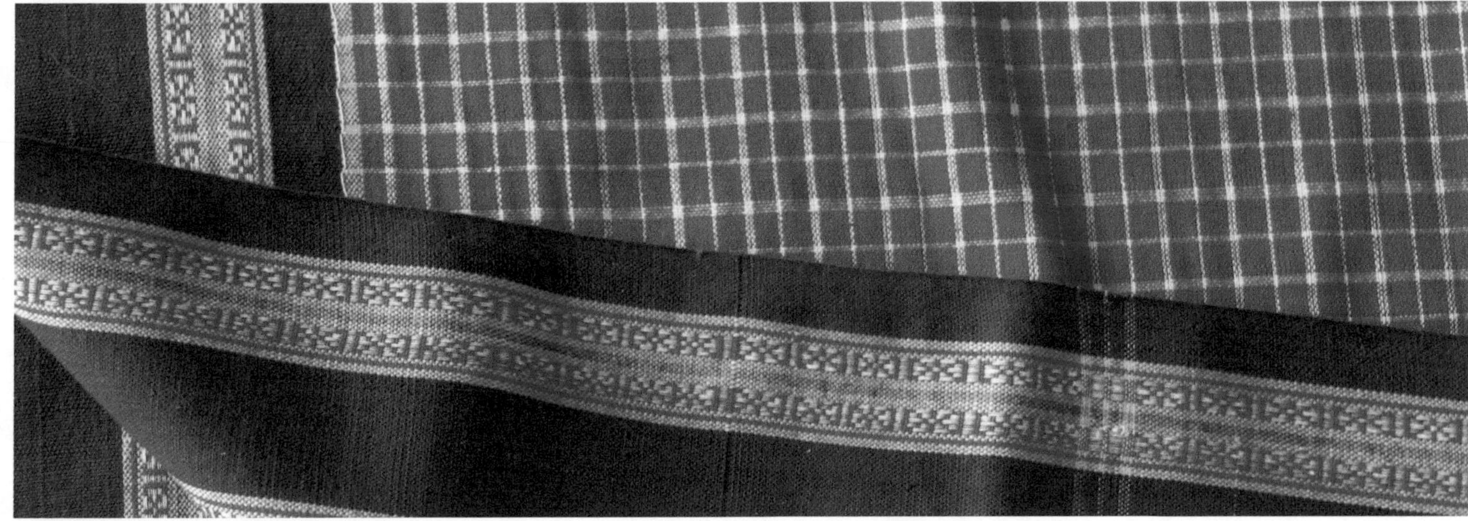

KERALA

KASAVU

Classic chic

या कुन्देन्दुतुषारहारधवला या शुभ्रवस्त्रावृता
या वीणावरदण्डमण्डितकरा या श्वेतपद्मासना।
या ब्रह्माच्युतशंकरप्रभृतिभिर्देवैः सदा वन्दिता
सा मां पातु सरस्वती भगवती निःशेषजाड्यापहा॥

(Lyrics of the Saraswati Vandana Shloka in Sanskrit)

This well-known Sanskrit shloka (verse), which I have chanted everyday since I was a kid, is dedicated to Goddess Saraswati. It describes the Hindu goddess of learning, knowledge and the arts - seated on a white lotus, pristinely beautiful, holding a *veena* (a stringed musical instrument), draped in a lovely white saree with a golden border. This is also almost exactly how she is depicted in pictures and paintings, including the wooden-framed one in my parents' house, that I used to pray to.

That white saree with a golden border reminds me of the Kasavu saree, typical of the western coastal state of Kerala. The thought of Kerala, a long, narrow stretch of green land with bountiful backwaters, evokes a myriad pictures in front of the mind's eye - beautiful landscapes, delicious food served on green plantain leaves, flower carpets, and the traditional white-and-gold garments for both men and women. The combination of white and gold, irrespective of what fabric it is made in, cotton, silk or a mixture, looks elegant and pristine, just like the one that Goddess Saraswati is draped in. White and gold are both considered auspicious colors all over the south of India, due to the purity they convey, so the choice should not be surprising, but in a country obsessed with bold colors, this choice, especially on display during the annual festival of Onam, stands out.

If one thinks of the all-year-round scorching heat of Kerala, the choice of white cotton is a logical and practical one; the gold border adds an elegant, aesthetic and festive touch to it - voila, there you have the Kasavu. The Kerala Kasavu, originally known as the *Mundum Neriyathum*, is typically a two-piece cloth. The habit of wearing two pieces of cloth to drape the body can be traced back to ancient Aryan times where the *Vastra* and *Upa-vastra* (main garment and accessory garment) were the norm; Buddhists continued this tradition with the *Antariya* and *Uttariya*. The Kasavu blends this tradition into that of wearing one long piece of unstitched cloth as a saree - so you have both forms - the two-piece or the single long piece. Gold-rimmed borders were added by the royals of Travancore during the handloom industry revolution.

Kasavu sarees exude elegance and richness in their simplicity. Every Malayali woman (Malayalis are natives of Kerala) has at least one, and often several of these in her wardrobe. The material and designs vary over a wide range, making it available and affordable to the masses, but also giving ample scope for chic and classy designs, for those looking for exclusivity. The celebrated painter Raja Ravi Verma, who belonged to the city of Travancore in Kerala, has used the *Mundum Neriyathum* freely to adorn some of his beautiful female protagonists such as the Nair woman, *Mohini, Ahilya, Damayanti* and *Shakuntala*, and also of course, my favorite, Goddess Saraswati, immortalizing the beauty and elegance of the Kasavu.

features

Kasavus are woven on handlooms, a technique with a history of 300 years. The Shaaliyars successfully made an industry of it, as they wove this elegant garment on handlooms for the royal families of Travancore. There are four main centers for weaving the traditional handlooms of Kerala – Balaramapuram, Kuthampully, Chendamangalam and Kasaragod.

"Kasavu" actually refers to the *zari* used in the border of this saree, rather than the saree itself. The *Mundum Neriyathum* is traditionally white or off-white in color and consists of two pieces of cloth, which have a gold-colored stripe at the border known as *Kasavu kara* or the golden layer. The border can be in pure golden *zari*, copper coated or artificial. The piece of cloth that drapes the lower garment is called the *mundu*, the other one, worn as the upper garment, is the *neriyathu*. The *neriyathu* is worn over a blouse, with one end tucked inside the *pavadai* (petticoat) while the loose end is left hanging from the left shoulder, resembling the *nivi* saree draping style. Performers of Kerala's traditional dance form Mohiniyattam wear only Kasavu garments; it is also a popular choice for other dance forms such as Kaikottikali, where performers wear Kasavu sarees with traditional red blouses.

Traditional *Mundu* sarees are distinctive with their white or light-colored (beige, cream or off-white) base with simple lines and luxurious (*kara*) golden borders. The material is usually fine, woven cotton or cotton-silk, though they are also made in pure silk or tissue silk. Whichever the material, the Kasavu offers one of the most comfortable, practical yet beautiful and elegant fashion choices in sarees, that can be worn for a wide variety of occasions. With the growing popularity of Kasavu sarees, embellishments like thread work, stones, sequins, or motifs on the *pallu* (such as peacock motifs) or other design elements like hand-painted murals (such as those inspired by the *Kanikonna* flower) are being added to the traditional design, to bring variety as well as color and pattern to its timeless elegance. These new trendy designs also look good, but for me, in the case of the Kasavu, old is indeed gold.

Traditional Mundu sarees are distinctive with their white or light-colored (beige, cream or off-white) base with simple lines and luxurious (kara) golden borders.

TAMIL NADU

KANJIVARAM

Resplendent radiance

"Fashions fade, style is eternal."
—Yves Saint Laurent

There are many style icons in the film world. The first style icon that I started following as a fan, and who was probably the first ever style icon in the Indian film industry, was Rekha, a celebrated actress and the golden goddess of Bollywood.

I have vivid memories of my teen admiration of and fascination with this beautiful diva, who was always perfectly turned out in her dazzling sarees. I soon learnt that these were traditional sarees of South India, called Kanjivaram sarees. I don't think I have seen anyone else carry the grand Kanjivaram as easily and naturally as Rekha does - seeing her in this beautiful drape is a visual treat.

I still remember my first shopping trip to buy Kanjivarams - it was for my cousin's wedding shopping that we visited the famous Nalli's saree shop on Bhulabhai Desai Road in Mumbai. This trip, which was my first time to feast my eyes on so many varieties of Kanjivarams, formally inducted me forever into the fan club of this luxurious and lustrous weave. My love for Kanjivaram sarees has only grown in the years since.

Kanjivaram sarees get their name from the city they were traditionally produced, Kanchi or Kanchipuram, a city close to Chennai in the southern Indian state of Tamil Nadu, known both for its temples and sarees alike. While Kanjivarams are rich in variety and creative designs, their default structure is the same across varieties and is defined by tradition. An original Kanjivaram is woven in lustrous three-ply pure mulberry silk (*murukku pattu*), and is embellished with real *zari*. Borders (*karai*), and *pallus* (*thalaippu*) are often in colors contrasting with the body color. Kanjivarams' bold use of color in solid and textured borders and beautiful patterns made with vivid silk yarn or tonal jacquard patterning on silk, create endless possibilities of design.

Kanjivaram flaunts a wide variety of materials, designs and styles that have evolved over time. Traditional sarees have heavy borders, but with the passage of time, these have given way to lighter versions as well. Soft pastel colors have come into the palette, and new materials are now being used. While pure gold and silver are used for the *zari* in a classic Kanjivaram saree, with changing times, silk and metallic threads have replaced gold and silver, and work of jacquard machines has replaced hand-work of artisans in many of the modern versions, making them more affordable while also broadening the variety.

A Kanjivaram saree is literally magic in silk. The sublime weaving, beautiful designs and motifs (both vintage and modern), the splendor of fabrics, *zari* and colors - all connect straight to the heart, making the lure of a Kanjivaram irresistible. Every element of this saree, whether traditional or contemporary, exudes refined craftsmenship. Its grace and glamor can adorn women's wardrobes not just for a lifetime but way beyond, as it is handed down as an heirloom from generation to generation. Little wonder that the Kanjivaram, the dazzling diva and undoubtedly the queen of silks, has reigned hearts of saree lovers for centuries.

features

The Kanjivaram's motifs are deeply rooted in the iconography of Dravidian cultural aesthetics. The great dynasties of the Pallava, Chola, Vijayanagar and Nayak kings left their majestic imprints on temple architecture and sculpture in Kanchipuram and its surrounding regions, and from there, onto the motifs and designs used in its sarees. The classic temple (*gopuram*) borders with *rudraksham* (holy beads) are a part of this connection, so are several common motifs like *hamsa* (swan), *kamala* (lotus), *kalpavriksha* (tree of life), *poorna-kumbha* (pot of abundance), *yanai* (elephant), *simha* (lion), *mayil* (peacock), *maan* (deer), *kili* (parrot), *iru thalai pakshi* (two-headed eagle), *yaali* (ubiquitous mythical creature), *kuyilkann* and *mayilkann* (eyes of the cuckoo and peacock).

The *udal* or base of the saree can be plain, with patterns, small or big. These could be the *butta* (coin pattern), *butti* (circular patterns) or other patterns such as *malli moggu* (jasmine buds), mango or paisley, *muthu* (pearl), *vaira oosi* or *vairam* (diamond needle or diamond pattern), *neli* (toe ring) or *pavunpet* (gold coin). *Kattam* (checks) and *vari* (stripes) are used so abundantly in weaving that it has given rise to an independent set of vocabulary to describe specific patterns created with these different designs.

The colors of the Kanjivaram are a fundamental design element, hence immensely important. The traditional Kanjivaram palette is made up of strikingly vibrant and brilliant jewel tones, with a broad color spectrum. The already vibrant colors are made even more radiant with *zari*, the finest gold thread that embellishes the saree, another integral feature of the Kanjivaram. *Zari* creates lustrous shades of every color, turning even a color as plain as white into a broad palette of shades including pearls, creams, vanillas and ivories with different levels of shimmer, each truly stunning.

Unlike other silk sarees, borders (*karai*) and *pallus* (*mundhanai or thalaippu*) of Kanjivaram sarees are not woven seamlessly with the body. They are attached. The border is attached to the body with an inter-locked weft technique called *korvai*. The woven attachment of *korvai* borders is one of the hallmarks of a classic Kanjivaram.

The woven attachment of korvai borders is one of the hallmarks of a classic Kanjivaram.

The pallu is attached using the *petni* technique, where weavers use the ancient craft of three-shuttle weaving and interlocking weft. This gives rise to different types of effects and patterns varying from a straight line to the more traditional *rekku* (spired temple) motifs that are locally referred to as "*thazamburekku*" (the *Kewra* flower).

ODISHA

BOMKAI

Balletic poise

India's rich artistic heritage is replete with native dance forms. As a child, I would ardently watch dance concerts that were commonly featured on television, either live or recorded. My mother, who had always wished that I learn a classical dance form, was happy to see this, only to discover later that my fascination was for the beautiful, colorful costumes worn by dancers, and not for their graceful dance steps. I could hardly remember any dance form names, but I could associate them with the type of sarees worn for each. Odissi was one of the first dance types I started to recognize by its costume - the brightly colored traditional Bomkai or Sambalpuri Oriya saree. So, while I never stepped into a dance school, my foray into sarees was encouraged and inspired in some ways by dance, some consolation to my mom whose wish for me to be a dancer will stay unfulfilled in this lifetime.

Odissi female dancers' sarees flaunt bright colors with patterned borders and intricate designs on some of the most traditional weaves of Odisha (formerly known as Orissa), a state in eastern India. The most commonly used types are Bomkai and Sambalpuri silk sarees. These are draped by dancers in a way that broad pleats of both the border as well as the *pallu* show in the front. This is such a clever drape that it not just enables flexibility of movement for the dancer while allowing the audience to see their delicate footwork, but also gives ample opportunity for them to display their beautiful *ghungroos* (dance anklets with metallic bells that ring with steps) and their gorgeous sarees. The luxurious pleats of the *pallu* and borders fan in and out as the dancer moves about, making a dance of their own alongside that of the dancer, each enhancing the other. My favorite visual is of an Odissi dancer sitting in the *chouka* position, when the pleats fan out their widest, lending exceptional beauty to this already graceful pose.

Odisha is known for its unique textiles with a distinctively native identity, quite unchanged over time. The reason is obvious - while northern India faced repeated invasions and consequent cultural influences from outside, Odisha, being isolated from the rest of India by mountain ranges on the west and the Bay of Bengal to the east, stayed relatively immune to and untouched by these. The ikat fabrics produced in Odisha are quite unique, flaunting indigenous techniques like *bandha kala* (tie-resist dyeing), a fine weaving and design method. *Bandha* or ikat textiles of Odisha are widely acknowledged for their intricate patterns, distinctive curvilinear motifs and the combination of ikat and relief texture created by supplementary warp and weft weaves. This texture is the biggest draw of these cotton and silk ikat textiles.

The Bomkai saree is an extraordinary confluence of two popular Orissa textile elements, namely ikat (called "*bandha*" locally) and embroidery work. Woven with the three-shuttle weaving process, the most charming part of this saree is the intricate *jaala*-patterned threadwork with bright, contrasting colors in its border and *pallu* designs. Traditional motifs and mythological stories can be seen in this exquisite weave from Odisha. Odissi is a sensual, lyrical and exceptionally graceful dance; the Bomkai adds to its charm, simultaneously elegant and magnificent.

features

Ikat is woven in many styles among weavers of Odisha. Odisha ikat silk sarees are made from fine-count silk yarns with vibrant colors in metallic finish, tie-dyed to perfection. Indigenously procured silk yarns are best suited for these sarees and have an excellent finish. When you go to purchase Odissi sarees, the range of exquisite weaves, embroidery and versatile designs that welcome you can be overwhelming - Aswini, Baghambari, Berhampuri, Dhalapathar, Dolabedi, Dongaria, Habaspuri, Nabakothi, Nuapatna, Pasapalli, Pattachitra, Sachipaar, Siminoi, Utkalaxmi are a few of the varieties available. Broadly, these can be classified into four categories - Bomkai, Sambalpuri, Khandua and tribal Kotpad cotton, each noteworthy for something special. The Khandua, for instance, a tie-dyed ikat silk saree variation woven in Nuapatna in the district of Cuttack, with its signature *pallu* of alternating lines with motifs in between, gets its importance because it is the type of saree offered to Lord Jagannath, the reigning deity of Puri. The Bomkai is a signature saree of Odisha, almost synonymous with this eastern state.

The border of a Bomkai with its trellis pattern of a basic diamond shape is its most prominent and distinctive attribute.

The Bomkai saree, also known as Sonepuri, originated in the Ganjam district of southern Odisha. It carries traditional Oriya motifs - *rukha* (pestle), *dambaroo* (hour-glass shaped drum), *karela* (bitter-gourd), *atasi* and *kanthi* phul (flowers), *macchi* (fish), *rui macchi* (carp-fish), *koincha* (tortoise), *padma* (lotus), *mayura* (peacock), *charai* (bird), *shankha* (conch shell), *chakra* (Konark wheel), dancing dolls and temple drawings are some of the more common ones. Of these, the fish motif is believed to be the most auspicious, a sign of success and affluence.

The four basic colors of black, white, red and yellow, traditionally used in Oriya sarees, are extracted from vegetable dyes (black from myrobalan, yellow from turmeric, dark red or maroon from lac, and *girmati* or light red from ochre treated with ghee). The border of a Bomkai with its trellis pattern of a basic diamond shape is its most prominent and distinctive attribute. Called *Mikta Panji*, it is made with the supplementary-warp model.

The diamond form is taken from motifs of *dalimba* (pomegranate corns) and *saara* (seeds) which are diamond-shaped beads halved vertically with dots within. These motifs are topped with a row of *kumbha* (temple spire) motifs. sea shells, wheels, *phoda kumbha* (a specific temple border needing two weavers) and *patli* (half-and-half pattern) borders are other common motifs in the borders of Odisha handloom sarees.

ANDHRA PRADESH

KALAMKARI

Kalam (pen) on cloth

Discovering new cultures is exciting, always making visits to new countries very interesting. It is not so often, however, that one learns about one's own culture when visiting a different country. That's how I discovered Kalamkari.

Knowing my interest in learning Mexico's history, Diana, my friend and neighbor, has spent a lot of time with me, introducing me to the diverse ethnic art, music, food and culture of Mexico. On one such occasion, at the impressive Neo-Gothic Museo Nacional de Historia in Bosque de Chapultepec in Mexico City, we had the pleasure to meet the artist whose canvas paintings were on display there. It was she who introduced me to and educated me about the history of not just Mexican canvas painting but also one type of Indian painting on canvas, called "Kalamkari". We had a long discussion about the art of story-telling on canvas, and the differences in Mexican and Indian styles of this art.

On my way out of the museum, I marveled about the fact that I had to go halfway around the earth from my country to discover this part of its rich story-telling heritage. I did not know at the time that this would not be the only time for this to happen.

The word "Kalamkari" or "*Qalamkari*" has Persian roots, and has two parts - "*kalam*" or "*qalam*" that means pen, and "*kari*" (pronounced as "*kaari*"), which means work or craftsmanship. When translated literally, Kalamkari means work or creation made with a pen. It is a form of painting on cotton fabrics with a *kalam* or pen. The pen in this case is made of bamboo - its hollowness allows space to fill in the color as ink, its tip is sawed sharp for the nib and it is pierced to allow regulation of the flow of color on the fabric. While this ancient craft used to be about simple drawings in the past, today it goes much beyond.

As with many other traditional Indian textile arts, the intricate techniques of Kalamkari have been passed down from one generation of artisans to the next for centuries. In the period between the thirteenth and nineteenth centuries AD, especially in the state of Andhra Pradesh, Chitrakathis (*Chitra* - picture, *Kathi* - story teller), who were entertainers that told stories with visual aids, started using large boards of canvas painted with plant-extracted dyes as stage backdrops for their plays. These were used like storyboards, with scenes from mythological epics depicted on them along with cultural texts, as the story was enacted in a play or expressed in a classical dance form like Kathakali. This is how Kalamkari was introduced into the cultural fabric of India, and soon made its way from canvas to cotton fabrics, evolving into an exquisite textile art form involving hand-painting or block-printing with traditional, natural vegetable dyes. Even in block-printing, artisans use hand-painting to bring out the finer details of the design, showing their art and creativity. In olden times, Kalamkari fabrics were a way to take mythological tales to the masses - often a whole story or episode or even a series of tales, especially from the epic of the Mahabharata, would be portrayed in Kalamkari works.

Every saree has a tale to tell, few do it as obviously as the Kalamkari.

features

Kalamkari, hailing from Andhra Pradesh, is not just a unique form of hand-painting, but has become a highly popular form of hand-painted or block-printed cotton textiles. It is an intricate and evolved art, involving up to twenty-three tedious steps of dyeing, bleaching, hand-painting, block-printing, starching, washing and more. The way this treatment is done and the quality of the mordant used determine the look and the luster of the final product, and hence are as important as the painting itself. As important as the art of painting itself, therefore, is the art of fabric treatment.

The Machilipatnam style of Kalamkari from Krishna district involves block-printing with hand-carved and hand-painted traditional blocks, while the Srikalahasti style from Chittoor district involves Kalamkari painting onto dyed fabrics. The latter is the more arduous of the two styles.

The blocks used in **Machilipatnam Kalamkari** have intricate detailing and are hand-painted before printing to get the right colors on the fabric. The block-printing process, which uses natural dyes with multiple rounds of soaking and dyeing, usually starts with just outlines (versus detailed line drawings). After the initial block-printing is done, the artisan adds minute finer details of the inner design using hand-painting.

In **Srikalahasti Kalamkari**, the cotton cloth is pre-treated - it is first thoroughly washed with water to remove starch and other oily substances. After drying, it is dipped into buffalo milk mixed with Myrobalan fruit dust, and then, after squeezing out the excess solution, it is dried again. Now the cloth is ready. On this, the initial drawing is done with charcoal pencil (made from burnt twigs of the tamarind tree) and then colored with a bamboo pen. Srikalahasti style of painting is known for its depictions of scenes from Hindu mythological epics and folklore.

Kalamkari is an intricate and evolved art, involving up to twenty-three tedious steps of dyeing, bleaching, hand-painting, block-printing, starching, washing and more.

With their traditional tools, Kalamkars bring out the magnificence and grandeur of deities and divine characters (including the Buddha) while also showing small and minute details of beautiful natural motifs like lotus, peacock and vines. The natural dyes and tools used in Kalamkari make this not just a very environment-friendly art, but also add to the richness of the shades and art forms that come to life on cotton, crepe or silk.

TELANGANA

NARAYANPET

Less is beautiful

Pune, one of the big cities of India about a hundred and fifty kilometers from the metropolis of Mumbai, is the cultural capital of the state of Maharashtra, steeped in history of Maratha royals and royal families. I have traveled to Pune many times with my family. On one such trip, we visited Theur (pronounced "*thay-oor*"), a village that sits at the confluence of three major rivers — Mula, Mutha and Bhima, on the outskirts of Pune. Here we visited the famous temple of Lord Chintamani, family deity of the Peshwas, who were among the most famous ruling dynasties of Maharashtra. I have beautiful memories of the temple, with its simple, serene ambience; I can still almost smell the gentle fragrance of incense burning in the temple, welcoming devotees in on the beautiful day. Shrimant Madhavrao Peshwa and his wife Ramabai, two beloved figures in Maratha history, cherished this temple in their lifetime. A picture depicting the young couple hung in the temple, showing Ramabai in a distinctive mango-yellow drape, that my mother told me, was a Narayanpet saree. Ignorant of its roots, I presumed "Narayan Peth" was one of the local markets in Pune, which are also called "peth"s. I was wrong. While the saree was intricately linked to Pune and its rulers, its roots lay far away.

Narayanpet is a small town on the border of the modern states of Telangana and Karnataka, which in Maratha times, was under the rule of the Marathas. It is said that Chhatrapati Shivaji, the most revered Maratha ruler, once camped for some time at Narayanpet during his travels. The royal camp had several craftsmen including weavers. When the royal camp shifted, a few weavers stayed behind with the Chhatrapati's endorsement, and established the manufacturing and trade of silk weaves. The style of their weaves and designs was very distinctive, and earned fame as Narayanpet sarees. These traditional sarees are very popular in the state of Maharashtra, and are worn not just for special occasions, but also offered in worship to the eternal Goddess.

The Narayanpet saree is known for its distinctive design, light weight, durability, affordability and easy maintenance. It is also easily recognizable by its design of a plain or checkered base, a contrasting *pallu* and a signature border with standard small, geometrical, *zari*-woven design running alongside it. The design is at once simple and pretty, which along with the light weight of the saree and consequent ease of draping, enhances its appeal. The other speciality of these sarees is the range of distinctive colors, beautifully contrasted in body and borders.

Once a part of the royal patronage of the Marathas, the traditional grandeur and beauty of Narayanpet sarees has stood the test of time, winning hearts of women even to this day with their soft, light silk and lovely hues. Whenever I touch one of my Narayanpet sarees, the rustle of its silk takes me back to the Chintamani temple in Theur, where I was first introduced to it.

features

There are many types of sarees named after the place where they are woven, but over time, they started getting made in and around that area. Narayanpet sarees are however an exception to this - the entire weaver community involved in this art is located only in Narayanpet, a small town in Telangana, bordering Yadgir/Gulbarga districts of Karnataka, even after all these centuries. This art developed under Maratha patronage but over time the town of Narayanpet lost its link to Maharashtra and is now wedged in between the provinces of Karnataka and Telangana. The style of weaving shows the distinct influence of all three states.

The Narayanpet saree is woven in fine cotton, cotton-silk or pure silk. Fine Cotton sarees have a thread count of at least eighty. The production of silk Narayanpet sarees is quite unique - silk is mounted for up to eight sarees per loom and a big group or community works on it. Thus, not the standard seven yards but fifty-six yards of silk are mounted on the loom at a given time. Degumming makes the silk light and suitable for weaving. The actual weaving starts after the degumming, dyeing and drying processes are completed, and the saree is woven on a preset loom.

These sarees flaunt a wide spectrum of shades ranging from the earthy to the vibrant, rich and lustrous, with contrasting borders. The base saree, whether in pure cotton or pure silk, may be plain or with a pattern of small colored checks, but no other design or motif. The border is woven on both the sides of the saree running through its entire length. The size of the border on both sides is uniform, ranging from 3 to 5.5 inches, woven in strongly with eight threads. The weaving generates a small geometrical (normally triangular) temple design along the border, which is a signature of these sarees. Another distinctive feature of Narayanpet silk sarees is the presence of "*Theni pallu*" (arrowheads) without any other intricate designs. The *Theni pallu* or temple borders may not be present in cotton sarees.

The weaving generates a small geometrical (normally triangular) temple design along the border, which is a signature of these sarees.

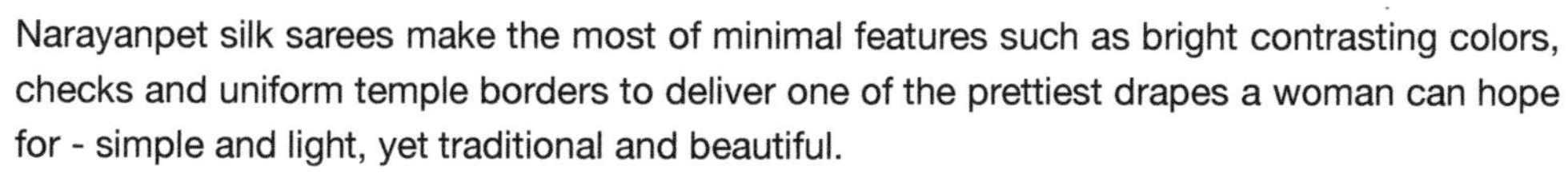

Narayanpet silk sarees make the most of minimal features such as bright contrasting colors, checks and uniform temple borders to deliver one of the prettiest drapes a woman can hope for - simple and light, yet traditional and beautiful.

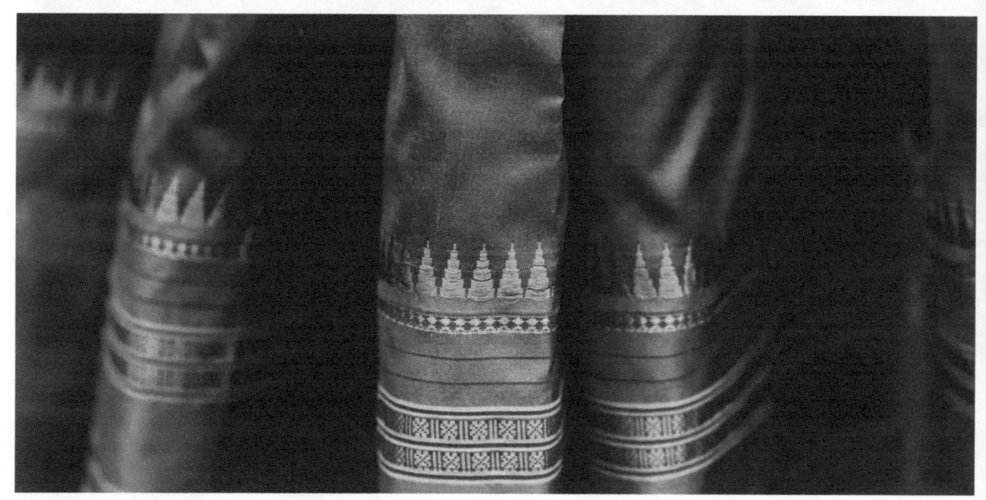

BIHAR & NEPAL

MADHUBANI

Folklore on fabric

It was a gorgeous day in Kathmandu, the capital city of Nepal. We were just back from the picturesque Pokhara valley, after filling our pot of memories with the breathtaking beauty of the Annapurna ranges and the serene tranquility of Lake Phewa. We were now making the best of our day and a half in Kathmandu by visiting sites.

There were three of us - our tour guide, a Japanese lady from the tour group and I. After seeing the famous Pashupatinath Temple and the tourist hotspot of Thamel, we dispersed off to look for souvenirs. We peeked into some art galleries, and some intricate, vibrant paintings caught my eye.

On enquiry, I discovered that these paintings represented the famous Mithila or Madhubani folk-art of India and Nepal. We then stumbled upon a beautiful handicraft shop just outside the Thamel area, specializing in cotton and silk clothing created by women's groups in Nepal, called "Local Women's Handicrafts", with a wide variety of silk souvenirs. Our tour guide noticed my interest in a beautiful stole in Tussar silk, hand-painted in vivid Madhubani style, and went on to give me my first lesson in Madhubani art.

Madhuban, literally meaning a sweet forest or a forest of honey ("*madhu*" means honey, "*banâ*" means forest), is an area occupying the northern part of Bihar through to the Mithila region of Nepal. The painting art from this region is the art form we are talking about - called Madhubani or Mithila painting. Madhubani painting is an ancient style of painting that hails from two and a half millennia ago. Surprisingly, the existence of this art form remained relatively unknown to the outside world until 1934, when an earthquake brought houses along the India-Nepal border tumbling down, unveiling paintings made on internal house walls, exposing this art to the world.

This wall art was in vogue widely in this region, kept alive by womenfolk who mastered and practiced it to beautify their modest homes. Paintings on paper, canvas and fabric are all more recent developments, which are referred to as Madhubani or Mithila art. Madhubani painting is done with different tools - twigs, brushes, nib-pens, matchsticks, brushes or just fingers. They are made freehand (without a preliminary sketch), using beautiful patterns. Borders are embellished with natural motifs and floral patterns, while blank spaces are filled in with further patterns or colors.

As our tour guide was bringing me up to speed thus, the Japanese lady also chipped in with the knowledge she had gained from her recent visit to the Mithila Museum in Tokamachi. Her interest in the art opened my eyes to the name and fame it has earned internationally, as Madhubani artists now display their art not just on canvas and fabric but also many other surfaces like fiberglass and metal.

Travel opens the mind to new places and new cultures. Ironically, for me it also opened a window to cultural aspects from my own homeland. I had already discovered the colorful Kalamkari in this manner during my Mexico visit. I left that shop in Thamel that day with two bags and a heart full of tributes and admiration for Madhubani - another art form of my country that I had to travel outside of it to discover.

features

Madhubani art form is a celebration of nature - heavenly bodies like the sun and the moon, natural motifs like flowers, leaves and plants like bamboo, *tulsi* (basil) are found aplenty in these designs; equally, motifs like those of the fish, peacock, parrot, elephant, turtle, snake and many others show up. These natural motifs are a main characteristic of this artform, another is its two-dimensional imagery with human figures that are mostly abstract. Themes used by Madhubani artists are often mythological, such as Lord Krishna playing his iconic flute, *bar-kanai* (bride and bridegroom), the wedding of Ram and Sita, the *raas-leela* of Radha and Krishna, and so on. Despite common themes, each painting is unique in beauty and style.

A mandala, literally meaning a circle in Sanskrit, is a complex abstract design that represents the connection between our inner worlds and outer reality.

Madhubani art has five distinctive styles, namely *Bharni, Katchni, Tantrik, Godna* and *Kohbar. Bharni* is one of the most famous, where the subject is outlined in black while enclosed areas are filled out with vibrant colors. On the other hand the *Kachni* style, which uses only one or two colors, uses delicate fine lines to fill in the blank spaces. Fine details and light-shade effects are created with drawing techniques like hatching (parallel lines) and stippling (dots). *Tantrik* style painting depicts only religious texts and characters while *Godna* (tattoo) work features *mandala's*. A *mandala*, literally meaning a circle in Sanskrit, is a complex abstract design that represents the connection between our inner worlds and outer reality. *Godna* paintings are made mostly in black, with very little color. The outlines and inner filling are made by bamboo pens mostly with lampblack ink. Design compositions mostly include rows and concentric circles of flowers, fields, animals, figures and spirits. The *Kohbar* painting is filled with rich details and typically drawn on walls using earthy colors.

Sarees with Madhubani painting are generally made with Tussar silk. Outlines made from rice paste are used to frame brightly colored designs. The colors used here are mainly made from plants or other natural sources, like litchi leaves or turmeric for yellow color, *kusum* flower juice for red, *gaur* for brick red, rose petals for pink, *har-singaar* for saffron orange, *sikkat* for blue, french beans or apple leaves for green, *mehndi* or *henna* for brown and rice powder for white and soot for black.

MADHYA PRADESH

MAHESHWARI

Understated allure

Maheshwar in Madhya Pradesh is a small town off Indore, which I visited during one of my India trips. As I waited for my flight out of Indore's Devi Ahilya Airport, my mind was full of memories of the beautiful sites I had visited and thoughts of Maharani Ahilyabai - the beloved queen of this province from a few centuries ago, whose larger-than-life aura can be felt in this town even today. Maharani Ahilyabai, who hailed from the Holkar dynasty of Maratha rulers, left an imprint on my mind as a remarkable woman who was way ahead of her times, revered by her subjects not just for her immense courage, bravery and able leadership but also for being a kind, humble and humanitarian ruler. Her palace, the Ahilyeshwar Temple and the beautiful Narmada *ghat* (pronounced as "*ghaat*", meaning stairs leading into the river water), all built during her times, are tourist attractions to this day.

Other than thoughts of Rani Ahilyabai, my mind was full of images of the beautiful Narmada *ghat*. The sight of the huge steps leading down to the serene flow of the mighty Narmada, especially in the quiet hours of the morning, was beautiful and peaceful. The perfectly symmetrical architecture of the steps gives it a look of a patterned design from a distance. I remembered seeing that pattern before - in the designs of sarees my paternal grandma wore. I remember those sarees as relatively simple ones with small checks all over, with narrow *zari* borders and with plain *pallus* sporting a striped pattern. At festival celebrations or weddings in Marathi families in my grandma's time, nine-yard sarees of this type were quite common. This type of saree, commonly called the Indori saree (for obvious reasons) in Maharashtra, is one of the many types of sarees hailing from Maheshwar - another gift to this province and its people by Ahilyabai.

Ahilyabai developed Maheshwar into a center of handloom fabrics, bringing weavers from around the Malwa region to settle here. The Maheshwari saree was born through their creativity, with weavers drawing inspiration from elaborate designs and ornate carvings on the temples and fort in Maheshwar. The Maharani was a big patron of these sarees and fabrics which she not only used herself but also gifted to visiting dignitaries, a move that took the reputation of Maheshwari handloom to distant parts of India and abroad. It may very much be the impact of her personality that kept this saree understated yet fine and elegant, with its use of earthy colors, moderate contrasts, simple designs and minimal, muted *zari* used only in its borders and *pallu*. Consequently, the saree looks gorgeous in its classy and effortless grace, reflecting the personality of Ahilyabai.

features

The timeless influence of Maheshwar architecture shows in the designs of Maheshwari sarees, with more linear patterns than motifs used in the design. Even in their simplest form, which have a plain, checkered or striped body in solid color, and a narrow, colored border minimally embellished with *zari*, these sarees exude a classy look. One unique feature of this type of Maheshwari is its special border that can be used inside-out or upside down, due to its perfectly symmetrical and fully reversible border. This border is fondly called "*bugadi*" (an earring that can be worn either side up). The use of *zari* and *kinaari* is also unique to Maheshwari sarees, with the border featuring simple patterns such as *karnphool* (leaves and flowers), *chattaai* (mat), *chameli ka phool* (jasmine flower), *eent* (brick) and *heera* (diamond), all of which may be traced back to the detailing on the walls of Maheshwar Fort.

Even in their simplest form, which have a plain, checkered or striped body in solid color, and a narrow, colored border minimally embellished with zari, these sarees exude a classy look.

The saree that is known as the Indori saree in Maharashtra is one of the traditional design patterns of Maheshwari sarees in pure silk. This saree features a *pallu* with a standard design of five stripes, two white and three colored, alternately placed. This used to be a very lightweight, all-silk weave; but an invention of the last century is the use of cotton in the warp, which has now become the norm.

These sarees flaunt many different types, based on both colors and patterns - *Chandrakala, Baingani Chandrakala* (both with plain bodies), *Chandratara, Beli* and *Parbi* (with stripes or checks on the body).

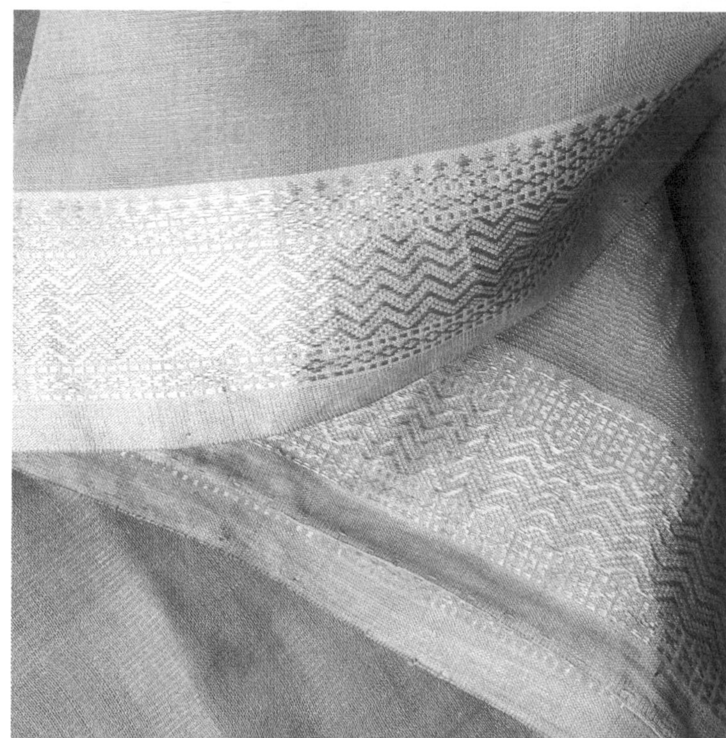

RAJASTHAN

KOTA DORIYA

Ethereal elegance

Words cannot express the pleasure I feel when I wear my mother's sarees - I feel so happy that I cannot stop smiling. I have a few of my mother's sarees in my wardrobe. My mother took great care of her sarees. Not all her sarees were expensive, but each was specially chosen for its distinct weave, show-casing her refined taste in classic and ethnic aesthetics. Some of the types are now rare to find. She has always believed that sarees are not to be kept unused; they need to be draped and loved. The more you wear them, the longer they last. No better example of this than a beautiful saree that adorned her ward-robe and now adorns mine - a coffee-black Kota.

Among my mom's sarees was this beautiful piece that came to her in her wedding trous-seau. An intricately woven piece, it had fine checks and shimmering *zari* in its weave, contrasting with its dark body color. In the many family events and special occasions that she donned it, she looked lovely in this ornate piece. In spite of all the glittering *zari* work on it, her Kota saree always felt light-weight and chic. I always loved this saree and wore it often, completely unaware of its origin or value, and I must admit now that I was not too careful about how I used it then. One day, my mom sat me down to share her saree story; that's how I got to know about the roots of the Kota saree and about the value of this piece. After that, I was more careful in handling it, and was secretly happy that I had inherited my mother's exclusive taste in sarees. I have treasured and preserved this saree with care, and worn it lovingly many more times since, often gazing with amazement at its stylish, diapha-nous, luster that has not faded even a bit, though this saree is older than me!

Very little has been written about Kota sarees, which are popularly known as Masuria in Kota and Kota Doriya (or Doria) outside the state of Rajasthan. The word "*doriya*" means thread. The square checks in the pattern, referred to as "*khats*", form one of the distinguishing features of the Kota Doriya fabric. A square comprising fourteen yarns, eight of cotton and six of silk, makes the most common *khat* in Kota Doriya. Approximately 300 to 350 *khats* constitute the width of the authentic handloom saree. The final fabric gets its delicate proper-ties from this very feature.

This almost weightless, sheer, translucent fabric is very popular for its gossamer feel and corded texture. Its airiness makes it very comfortable to wear in hot and humid summers. Kota sarees often have embroidery or patches in the body and/or border, giving each piece an individual and unique look and feel. A Kota saree makes a great choice for a stylish look at work as much as for a casual evening with friends.

My mother's love for sarees is unabated to this day, and I believe it has come into me in inheritance. Her beloved Kota Doriya saree is a priceless treasure that will always have a special place, both in my heart and my wardrobe.

features

Some say that Kota Doriya sarees originated in Mysore. It was in the late seventeenth century that Maharao Kishore Singh, a general in the Mughal army, brought weavers of this fabric from Mysore to Rajasthan. Since then, Kota Doriya weaving practice became more entrenched in the Kota district of southeast Rajasthan, primarily in Kaithoon, and its nearby villages. These weavers used to be called "*masurias*" and the Kota Doriya sarees have since been called as Kota Masuria sarees.

An authentic Kota Doriya saree typically has 1400 to 1500 *khats* or uniformed square checks in the length and 300 in the width of its sheer, light fabric, typically woven in fine silk, cotton or a blend of both. Kota silk-cotton sarees get their strength from the base of cotton and shine and transparency from silk.

Kota Doriya is woven on traditional, age-old pit-looms that use the throw-shuttle technique. Peg- warping is used mostly for Kota Doriya, where pegs are placed along the full length of the yarn so as to get a continuously criss-crossed set of two yarns for weaving. Onion juice and rice paste are applied to the yarn - a unique feature of the Kota Doriya. Rice makes the yarn strong and less brittle while onion juice ensures that its softness and lustrousness is wash-resistant and long-lasting.

Kota Doriya sarees are woven in three different styles: basic, block-printed and *zari*. Beautiful, creative embellishments are added, making them unique and varied, a saree-lover's delight. The traditional Kota Doriya is white or beige in color, with five shades of white seen most commonly, namely conch-shell, sea-foam, jasmine, moon and cloud. Technology has supplemented the natural dyeing process in recent times, to make bright hues like pomegranate, purple, red, turquoise, lapis-blue, black, turmeric-yellow and saffron possible. On the Kota fabric, these colors give a fairy-like brightness and lightness, burnishing its brilliance and elevating its elegant, ethereal look.

An authentic Kota Doriya saree typically has 1400 to 1500 khats or uniformed square checks in the length and 300 in the width of its sheer, light fabric.

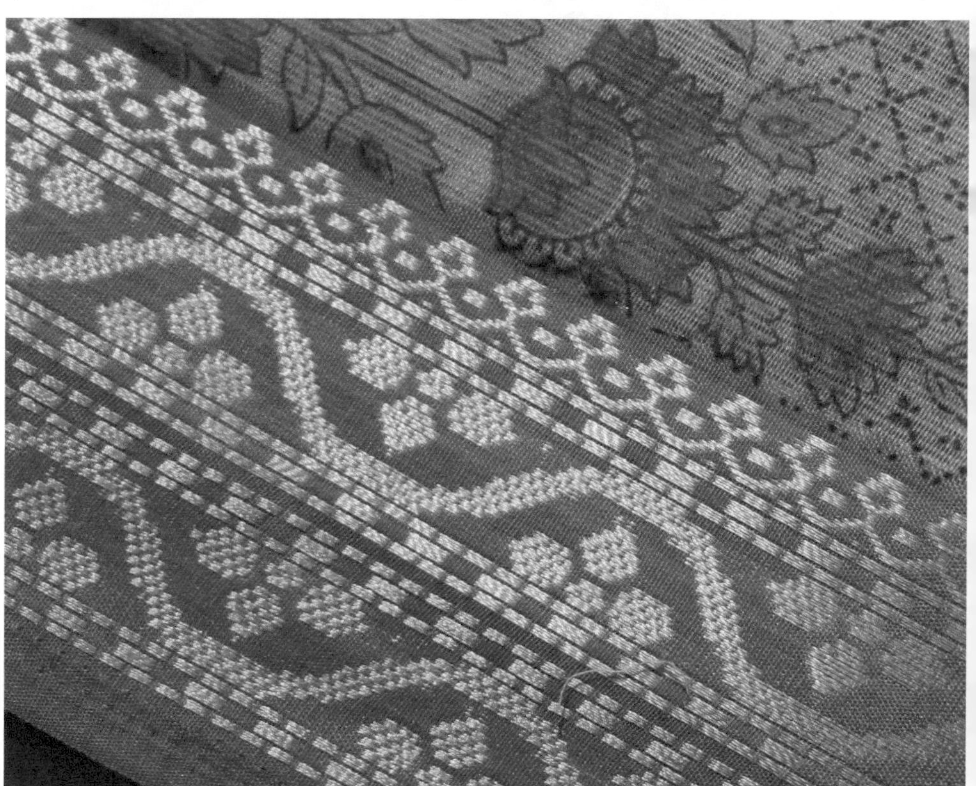

KARNATAKA

MYSORE SILK

Lustrous luxuriance

Of all four seasons, I love autumn the most. Trees suddenly seem to be in blossom with the color of drying leaves, almost in anticipation of the upcoming festivities in India. I always look forward to the country gearing up for the colorful festivals of Navratri and Diwali. It was in the fall one year that I visited Mysore, the city of palaces in the southern Indian state of Karnataka. The visit to the huge monolith of Nandi (the divine bull in Hindu mythology) atop a hill and the evening spent outside Sri Chamundeswari temple were both very memorable. The beautiful memory of the hazy skies of Mysore that were turning dark as the sun set, while *diyas* (oil lamps) being lit in the temple were slowly spreading their serene light, is etched in my mind forever. Shining bright in this tranquil moment was the charming idol of Goddess Chamundeswari, ever so resplendent in the Mysore silk saree draped around Her.

Mysore is known for many things - its royal heritage, its sandalwood and its silk. The history of Mysore silk can be traced back to Tipu Sultan, the ruler of Mysore in the 1790s. Enchanted by the silk cloth gifted to him by the ambassador from the Qing Dynasty's royal court in China, he sent a delegation each to Bengal and China, with the sole purpose of sourcing silkworms for cultivation. As a consequence, sericulture came into Mysore, and within a century of that, the kingdom of Mysore became one of the country's top silk producers, while its glimmering silk became a signature symbol of Maharajas and Sultans of Mysore.

Mysore silk as a fabric is loved for some very unique combinations of qualities that are quite rare - muted elegance despite its trademark sheen and *zari*, a lovely fall despite its feather-lightness, and a non-crush texture despite its butter-soft feel. Unlike other South Indian sarees, which are usually heavy and also have a lot of embroidery, Mysore silk sarees in their classic form are light and minimalistic in design, with simple, delicate *zari* borders and *pallus* that use only *zari* lines for design. Yet they are unmatched in the rich and easy elegance they exude. Little wonder that they are such a popular choice.

The variety and range of Mysore silk is truly vast. "Mysore silk" is a collective term used for an aggregation of silk types - crepe, semi-crepe, *zari*-border printed crepe, and georgette. Of these, Mysore crepe-de-chine, commonly known as georgette silk, is the most sought after. Apart from all the unique qualities of this saree already mentioned, it boasts of one of the best silks in this genre and an unparalleled range of color palette.

My very first saree was a bluish gray Mysore Crepe silk, with a black *zari* border. Mysore silk is also the first choice of my mother-in-law; no surprise then that many of her gifts to me were Mysore silk sarees. The understated beauty of this saree never ceases to amaze, making it an eternal favorite for both of us.

features

Karnataka state is the leading producer of silks in India, accounting for close to half of the country's mulberry silk production in 2020. In the beginning of the nineteenth century, inspired by Queen Victoria's celebration festivities in Britain, Maharaja Krishna Raj Wadiyar IV ordered thirty-two power looms from Switzerland to set up a silk manufacturing unit in Mysore. This was the beginning of machine-made silk sarees in India. Sericulture blossomed under his reign as the unit's capacity progressively increased to a hundred and seventy looms. He established the country's first silk manufacturing unit in 1912 – the Mysore Silk Weaving Factory. The patent and brand of Mysore Silk sarees is now owned by the Karnataka Silk Industries Corporation (KSIC), a government enterprise, known for their high quality Mysore silk sarees woven from the finest silk with pure gold *zari*.

The assurance of the premium *zari* used, the solidity of color and the sheen of the finest quality of silk are hallmarks of KSIC Mysore silk sarees. The base silk fabric is dyed in a single color and is kept plain without any patterns; this makes the intricate *zari* work on the borders stand out. The *zari* used in these sarees is procured from Surat in Gujarat, and uses real silver (65%) and 24-carat gold (0.65%), the secret of its real golden luster. This also makes it one of the most expensive sarees. Such is the strength of the pure *zari* on an authentic Mysore Silk saree that it does not fade, become dull or tarnish, even after repeated wear. Each KSIC saree has a distinct mark, guaranteeing authenticity and quality. The combination of high quality and beauty make the charm of this saree irresistible.

Mysore silk sarees sport a lavish color palette. While the traditional hues of orange, red and green are always popular, even modern pastel shades like lilac, coffee-brown and elephant-gray look beautiful on this fabric. The main embellishment of the classic Mysore silk saree is *zari* in linear patterns. Its modern avatar may also have motifs like mango *buttis* or floral borders added, but in modest measure relative to other traditional silk saree types.

This royal weave is definitely a heirloom that can traverse generations, retaining its status as a favorite through ages.

The assurance of the premium zari used, the solidity of color and the sheen of the finest quality of silk are hallmarks of KSIC Mysore silk sarees.

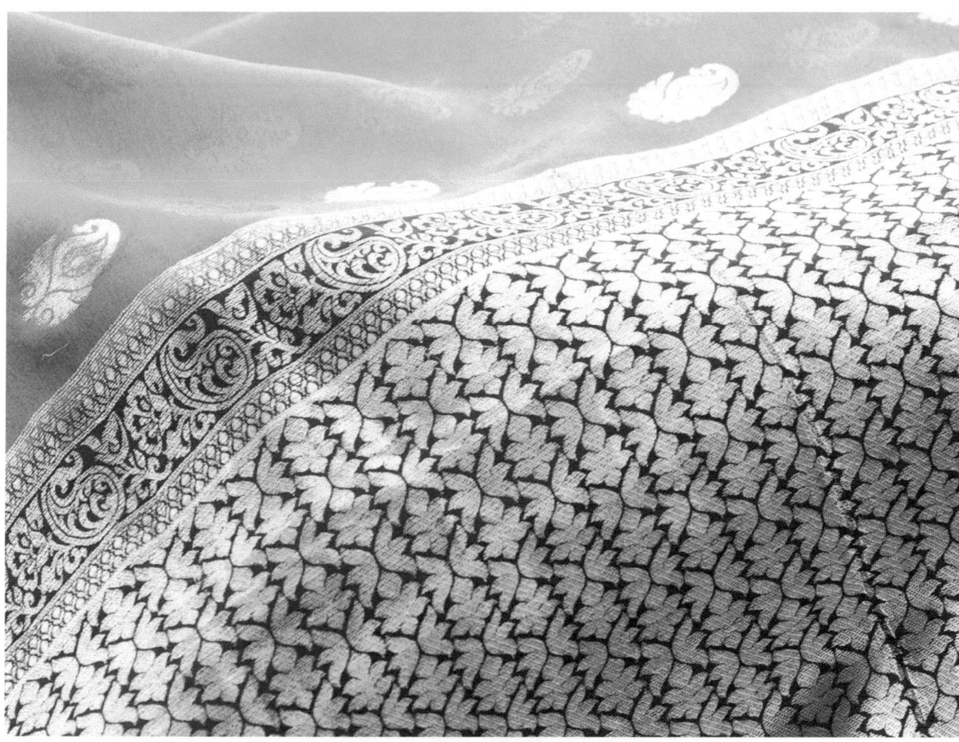

JAMMU & KASHMIR

THE PASHMINA

Breathtaking beauty

कितनी खूबसूरत ये तस्वीर है | मौसम बेमिसाल बेनज़ीर है |
ये कश्मीर है, ये कश्मीर है ||

(Translation of this song written by Anand Bakshi, from the Hindi movie Bemisal:
What a beautiful picture this is. The weather here is unparalleled, unique.
This is Kashmir, it's Kashmir)

This famous song from a Hindi movie describes very simply and aptly the lure of the Kashmir valley. With its serene, scintillating natural beauty, it is hailed as one of the most beautiful places on this planet. The picturesque landscapes of Kashmir in summer on the backdrop of the mighty Himalayas, featuring expansive lush green valleys, placid lakes and the unique vegetation of walnut and maple trees, can take your breath away with their beauty. Little surprise that such beauty has inspired unique art in this area, showing up in various forms including exquisite types of Kashmiri embroidery commonly used in Pashmina shawls, *Phirans* (Kashmiri *kurtis*) and sarees. Kashmiri embroidery is a treat to the eyes – opulent in its stunning designs yet elegant due to use of only colors without *zari*, sturdy in strength yet delicate in appearance, beautiful in looks yet appropriate for the weather.

Kashmiri sarees are a trend in the world of fashion today. Yet not much is known about these sarees. Spellbound by an exquisite Kashmiri saree that I received as a gift, I researched about this type, and discovered that Kashmiri embroidery is much more versatile than the limited impression I had of it upto that point. Kashmiri sarees are generally made of Pashmina silk (70% Pashmina and 30% silk) with distinctive heavy embroidery. The lovely designs made in intricate thread-work are inspired by nature, giving a unique look befitting the beauty of Kashmir.

Kashmiri hand-work on fabric includes both embroidery and weaving. Kashmiri embroidery, called *kashida*, has several varieties, the most widely used being Sozni, Aari and Tilla. These mostly use simple stitches such as the satin, stem, chain and long/short stitches, with occasional use of the herringbone, button-hole and darning types. The *jaali* or open latticework produces a lace-like effect. Woven Kashmiri textiles called Kaani normally use Pashmina silk to make a saree or shawl. They are also available in regular mulberry silk, bringing the prices down to more affordable levels.

Kashmiri art, just like its language, is heavily rooted in Persian influence. The word "*pashmina*" in Persian language means "made from wool", while in Kashmiri, it means soft gold, an apt name representing the gentle texture combined with its high value. Similarly, the word "*kashida*" is Persian, meaning embroidery or drawing.

The quality of the fabric, its intrinsic softness, impeccable embroidery work and unique, elaborate motifs on Pashmina silk give Kashmiri sarees not just a unique and elegant appeal but also a high price tag. While not as opulent as some of the *zari*-work sarees, they can be as or more luxurious, and would be some of the most treasured possessions in the wardrobe.

features

Authentic pashmina shawls and sarees exude luxury, as they are handwoven from the finest quality cashmere wool (*pashm*). Pashmina yarn is harvested from the downy undercoat of three breeds of Pashmina goats, namely the *Changthangi* or Kashmir Pashmina goat, the *Chegu*, and *Chyangara* or Nepalese Pashmina goat. These elusive creatures can be found at 14,000 feet of elevation or higher, in the Himalayan mountain ranges. The practice of *kashida* embroidery began in the early eleventh century and flourished over time, to become a hot favorite with aristocracy and royalty, earning its place as one of the most elite forms of embroidery.

Kaani embroidery is woven on the loom itself in the body of the fabric while Aari, Sozni and Tilla use hand-embroidery made on top of ready fabric.

The Persia-inspired, distinctively traditional Kashmiri embroidery motifs include *gulab* (rose), *badam* (almond), *sarav* (Cypress), *kev posh* (root flower), *gul-e-noor jehan* (Empress Noor Jahan's favorite flower), *gulabkan* (roses), *mazaar posh* (meadow wildflower), *marder* (snake-like forms), *gulkar* (flowers), *ragas chinar* (maple leaf), *pamposh* (lotus blooms), *sosan* (Iris), *dachh* (vine), *sumbal* and *yemberzal* (hyacinth and narcissus), *dainposh* (pomegranate), along with many other twigs and trees.

Like all ancient crafts, Kashmiri textiles are created using traditional methods, based on which we can look at four types - Aari, Sozni, Kaani and Tilla. Kaani embroidery is woven on the loom itself in the body of the fabric while Aari, Sozni and Tilla use hand-embroidery made on top of ready fabric.

Kaani (weaving): Jamawar Kani or Kaani is Kashmiri thread-work woven in the fabric itself. "*Kaani*" is a Kashmiri word that describes the small wooden sticks used as tools on the loom while weaving to create eclectic patterns. Weaving is meticulously regulated by a coded pattern, known as the "*taleem*", which is a coded syntax or special script for communicating design specifications. The person who creates the *taleem*, called a "*naqash*" (Arabic origin word meaning "an artist"), is a master artist and an essential flag-bearer of this ancient craft. The *naqash* not only develops the design but also transfers it on to wooden blocks, which are then used for weaving. The *taleem* technique was first used in Kaani shawls and subse-

quently adapted to carpet-weaving. While the *taleem* contains all the information needed by the craftsman, to know what the design looks like, the artist has to embroider or weave it first line by line. A saree fully hand-woven in Jamawar Kaani weave is very colorful and intricate.

Tilla (embroidery): This type of embroidery work is found on women's cloaks (*pheron*), shawls and *salwar kameez* (local dress). It is done using imitation gold and silver thread or fine copper thread. Designers have begun to catch on to this style of embroidery for use on borders and *pallus* for sarees.

Aari (embroidery): This is a Kashmiri specialty, made of fine, concentric rings of chain stitch using a special hooked needle known as "*aarikamr*", which is similar to a crochet needle (*aari*). Each previous loop is held by the subsequent one, to make a chain effect. Aari is the most common embroidery we see on Kashmiri garments. There are two main types of Aari embroidery – *Poskar*, which has more than three colors of thread and full-bloomed flower designs. *Raskar*, which has less than 3 colors of thread and flower bud designs.

Sozni (embroidery): Sozni, also known as "*Sozankar*", is a graceful and delicate embroidery, mostly done on Pashmina fabric. The word "*sozni*" means needlework. This fine embroidery is done with stitches in a bright, single-colored thread. The designs are mostly in paisley and floral patterns. A single-sided embroidery pattern is called *Aksi*, while the same work done on both sides is called *Dorukha*.

GUJARAT & TELANGANA

PATOLA & POCHAMPALLY

Geometric grandeur

Some fabrics can be easily identified with the countries they come from because they are advertised and celebrated by their parent countries in different ways - one common way is on costumes and uniforms. Air India, India's national air carrier, has used different types of sarees for uniforms of their women crew and staff. The current version at the time of writing this book flaunts specially designed Pochampally silk, one of the most evolved and refined weaves of India.

Kamaladevi Chattopadhyay, freedom activist and social reformer, played a pivotal role in the revival of India's handicrafts and handlooms. Her enormous contributions to Indian performing arts, handicrafts and traditional textiles are remembered with immense gratitude. As per legend, during one of her travels in the country, Kamaladevi was given a wet cotton towel called Telia Rumal to drape around her head to beat the summer heat. Mesmerized by the beautiful design and texture of this cloth, she drove through the scorched Andhra countryside to track down its weavers. She met them and placed the first order for a few sarees to start a business with them. One thing led to another, ending in her sending some of those weavers to Gujarat and Varanasi to re-train themselves in ikat designs and silk weaving. Thus began the revival of an age-old weave in India - the Pochampally and Telia Rumaal ikat weaves.

From the ancient weave of ikat (also called ikkat or ikhat) came two types of contemporary styles - the Patola and the Pochampally - both vibrant and colorful without much gold or *zari* inlay. Patola sarees are woven in Rajkot and Patan (state of Gujarat) while Pochampally sarees hail from Bhoodan Pochampally and Puttapaka (state of Telangana). Many weaves in India and the world trace their roots back to the ikat, but hardly any can claim the grandeur that the Patola/Pochampally exude with their unique silk textures and colors. Both originating from the ikat, Patola and Pochampally have several points of resemblance while still having their unique features. Both are laborious weaves using specially dyed threads which are so finely made that they give an appearance of designs printed on the fabric. They differ, however, in the silk quality used as well as the design styles and patterns. For instance, Pochampally sarees which usually have full or partial ikat in the base use different motifs and colors mixed and matched across the base fabric, while Patola sarees are typically woven in a single design that goes all over the fabric. Here are some of the popular types of this saree -

Rajkot Patola & Pochampally single ikat silk sarees use single ikat technique, leading to less complex designs, hence lower price tags (than the Patan Patola), making them a popular choice. The single ikat technique is used by artisans when the overall look is more important than the precision of patterns.

Telia Rumaal sarees use double ikat on mercerised cotton yarn, which is not only tied-dyed, but also treated with castor oil to give the fabric a characteristic sheen.

Patan Patola is the mother of all double ikat techniques. Intricate, colorful and gorgeous, **Patan Patola** ikat has the sharpest of all Indian ikat patterns, requiring extreme mathematical precision as much as vivid imagination and creativity. No wonder this technique is regarded by many as the ultimate manifestation of weaving perfection and the Patan Patola as one of the highest forms of textile art.

With such science and art both packed in, this glorious weave, painstakingly dyed, spun and woven to perfection by expert weavers, exudes energy and beauty whenever it is worn. Its geometric and high-precision patterns appeal to the engineer in me, while its rippling energy and color ensnare the saree-lover in me.

features

Ikat derives its name from an Indonesian word "*mengikat*" that relates to tying, knotting or binding a yarn or thread. It describes a textile that is handwoven using a warp and/or weft, from threads that are tied and resist-dyed. Though its origin is unknown, historically ikats are known to have been woven in India during the reign of King Kumarpal of the Solanki dynasty in the twelfth century, gaining prominence in handloom textile art in three major regions – Gujarat, Telangana, and Odisha. Over the years, these three regions developed their own styles of ikat weaving, each distinct in pattern and dyeing technique. Odisha ikats have an indigenous breadth of motifs and peculiar curvilinear patterns, and deserve a separate feature of their own. This article focuses on Patola and Pochampally sarees. The main feature of these sarees is the type of ikat technique used.

A combination of natural motifs with geometric shapes creates designs that simply cannot be imitated using any other technique.

Single ikat: In this technique, the design shows up either in the warp or in the weft. In warp-based ikat, warp threads are visible even before the weft thread is woven in. Only the warp is resist-dyed, such that the pattern is clearly visible on it even before it is woven. The weft, on the contrary, may be dyed with a single color or may be undyed. In weft-based ikat, the weft yarn produces visible dyed patterns as it is woven into the warp, in order to produce the final fabric. The process of weft-based ikat is more involved and time-consuming than warp-based ikat, requiring extreme attention to detail from the artisan, to continually adjust the weft for maintaining consistency and clarity of pattern. As in all tie-dye techniques, the more the number of ties and colors, the more intricate and elaborate the design. Sambalpuri, Pochampally, Rajkot Patola are all fine examples of Indian single ikat work.

Double ikat: In this more complicated technique, both the warp and the weft are resist-dyed (tied to resist the dye) and then woven together. The tie-dye technique uses knots on every thread, strategically tied to get the needed color and pattern. The same process is then repeated for other colors, making the dyeing process complex. The Patola loom is one of its kind - it is tilted to one side and requires two people to sit and work together on one saree. The weaving process is complicated too - one displaced thread can result in a visibly deformed pattern. A handful of master weavers carry this art on, using centuries-old traditional weaving techniques. Patan Patola and Telia Rumaal Pochampally are examples of double ikat work.

Patola sarees have an immensely rich color variation and great depth in the simplest of designs. A combination of natural motifs with geometric shapes creates designs that simply cannot be imitated using any other technique. While large, well-defined diamonds, hexagons, squares are common, *nari kunj, navaratna bhaat, pan bhaat* and *vohra gajji* patterns in a vibrant and perfectly symmetrical medley of red, green, yellow and off-whites, are some charming signature designs woven only in this saree.

UTTAR PRADESH

BANARASI

Mystical magnificence

Banaras - mystical, majestic, magnificent! The aura of this ancient city, also known as "The City of Light" or "Kashi" in Rigveda, is as present today as it was in every century before, attracting people from all over the world. The old name of this city - Varanasi - originates from names of two rivers Varuna and Assi, tributaries of the Ganges, which form its natural northern and the southern boundaries respectively. The four-kilometer distance between these two rivers is connected by eighty-eight *ghats* (pronounced as "*ghaats*" meaning steps leading down into the river water). The rivers, the temples on the banks, the *ghats*, and the boats plying from one to another form the quintessential picture of Banaras. But what goes beyond words and pictures is the spirituality of the place, which can only be experienced once you are there. Memories of a morning spent there on the *ghats* are still fresh in my mind.

The sun rising, as if to the tune of the morning *aarti* (ritual of worship usually offered with lights) on Assi Ghat, the mystical tranquility of the Ganges shimmering in the soft light of these nascent sunrays, and the beautiful *ghats* waking up slowly to this scene, all created a feeling of peace. The red in the horizon gradually turned to gold, lifting the veil of mist from the serene river banks, presenting a spectacular view of the Darbhanga Palace and the nearby Dashashwamedh Ghat. As I watched this from a wooden rowing boat, I could begin to understand why this place evoked human introspection on the journey of life from times afar.

While mystics debate topics of spirituality in the temples and *ghats*, just a stone's throw away, in the narrow by-lanes of Peeli Kothi, *kaarigars* (artisans) keep an ancient art alive, the art of hand-weaving Banarasi sarees. We walked around this area later that day. The stunning range of masterpieces of Banaras handloom that I saw that day opened my eyes and my senses to the rich heritage of this textile.

I remember being utterly besotted, as a child, by the richness of the Banarasi saree. I have fallen in love with it over and over again a thousand times since. Among the different design patterns, I love Katan silk Valkalam Banarasi sarees with their ornate *resham* borders and stunning *pallus* as well as the sumptuous Jamawar and Shikargah Banarasi sarees. A Kadhuan brocade Jangla Katan silk Banarasi saree is still one of the most unique and intricate handlooms I've ever worn. I never cease to be amazed at how easily it drapes, a luxurious masterpiece that, in my opinion, even the biggest couture houses cannot top.

I know that the variety of Banarasi sarees can easily feel overwhelming and beyond comprehension. But it is not that complex. Banarasi (or Benarasi) is a generic name for sarees from Varanasi - it spans a broad spectrum of weaving techniques, designs and patterns. Once one understands the different weaves, fabrics and patterns used, one begins to truly understand how combinations of the different features give rise to different varieties of sarees. The variety and names become more intuitive, and the complexity is demystified.

The spell that the Banarasi saree holds over saree-lovers is in many ways similar to the trance its parent city casts on devotees. While these sarees are available in different types of fabric, the Banarasi silk saree is especially known for its fine soft fabric, its gleam, the ease with which it can be draped and its grand look. The range of weaves, the gold and silver brocades filled with silk and *zari* alike, the intricate designs and patterns, all contribute to the timeless love for the Banarasi saree, making it one of the most favorite choices for wedding trousseaus and some of the most fondly treasured heirlooms passed on from generation to generation.

features

In the first millennium BC, Banaras rose to the status of an important center of art, culture, and education. In the fifth and sixth centuries BC, Banaras was a thriving center of exquisitely woven cotton fabrics. During the Mughal period (around the fourteenth century), weaving of brocades with intricate designs using gold and silver *zari* threads became the specialty of Banaras. Today, only brocade made in the six specified districts from the state of Uttar Pradesh, namely Varanasi, Mirzapur, Chandauli, Bhadohi, Jaunpur and Azamgarh districts, can be legally sold as Banarasi brocade.

The koniya motif (corner paisley) woven in the ornamental pallu is one of the most admired, difficult-to-weave motifs in brocade handloom.

Fabrics: While Banarasi sarees are made in a wide range of fabrics, some are more popular, for instance, Katan silk (one of the finest varieties of lustrous mulberry silk), Kora organza (light, sheer and degummed), Khaddi georgette (thinner and highly twisted pure silk) and Shattir (or *Shahteer*), in addition to simple cotton. The feel, fall and drape of each fabric is unique - Katan silk sarees have a stiffer drape as compared to the figure-hugging drape of Banarasi georgette sarees, while the organza has a diaphanous yet defined look to it.

Colors: Banarasi weaves have a rich and varied color palette, allowing for even subtle differences in shades of the same color. Colloquial color names originating from nature and food add an element of fun to the vocabulary. Where else would you find whites in shades of *kapursafed* (camphor white) to *motia* (pearl white), creams from *makkai* (creamy corn) to *subz kishmish* (young raisins), *gulabi* (pink), *surkh* (ruby red), *aasmaani* (sky blue), and so on.

Motifs: The versatility and adaptability of the Indian *kairi* (raw/green mango) can be seen through many design variants on different handwoven base fabrics. Traditionally the paisley is alternatively woven as a *butti* on Kora, *butta* in soft satin and beautifully combined with a lattice Kadhua Jangla pattern on pure katan silk. The *koniya* motif (corner paisley) woven in the ornamental pallu is one of the most admired, difficult-to-weave motifs in brocade handloom. Floral motifs abound in the Banarasi catalog. The glorious *gulaab* (rose), a symbol of love, is used extensively, while the tulip is frequently seen in borders with roses and

lilies. The multi-hued crocus and iris motifs are borrowed from Persian designs, while those of the lotus, *champa*, jasmine, hibiscus, *gainda* (marigold) and *guldaudi* (chrysanthemum) are all part of the Banarasi repertoire.

A signature design of the Banarasi is a continuous flower-and-vine pattern that runs along the saree in such a way that when draped, it looks like a beautiful creeper running up and along the drape, adding a special oomph to the wearer's look.

Weaves and classic patterns

Banarasi sarees are distinctive because of their multifarious weaving techniques, which are complex and intricate, with unique looks and features. To understand the types of Banarasi sarees, it is important to first understand these weaving techniques, which can be categorized into *Khinkhwab* (brocade), *Kadiya*l (interlocking) and *Minakari* (pronounced as "*meenakaari*").

Khinkhwab or Brocades: These rich woven fabrics are the most remarkable specialty of Banaras. On the basis of the design in the weaving process, Banarasi brocades are further classified into categories like Kadhuan or Kadwa, Phekwa (cutwork), Tanchoi, Tissue, & Vasket.

Kadhuan is one of the most sophisticated, intricate and exclusive of handloom weaving techniques, where each motif is painstakingly woven separately by inserting an extra weft. This is done with such finesse that the back of the fabric shows no loose or cut threads, only neat, clean ends with the yarn twisting back on itself. Using this technique, diverse motifs of different sizes, colors and textures can be woven on the same fabric, which is quite difficult to achieve otherwise. The fine Kadhuan weave is a hallmark of Banarasi weaving, and cannot be replicated on a powerloom.

Phekwa involves an extra weft that is run using a shuttle from selvage to selvage of the fabric, and is interlaced between the structural yarns, weaving motifs across the width. This technique leaves a float of threads on the reverse of the saree fabric, unlike those woven in the Kadhuan style. The floats are then either cut away to make it a cut-work saree or left as they are, if the motifs cover most of the base of the fabric. The **Katruan** (cut-work) style leaves a neater reverse side. The cutting has to be done with great precision and dexterity.

Tanchoi is a dense brocade weaving technique that involves a single or double warp and multiple (usually two to five) colored wefts, often of very close or similar shades. The pattern is in the weave itself, made by primary weft threads themselves, with no float on the reverse side. The result is an all-over brocade covering the entire fabric, looking like a self-design in the fabric itself. This technique is used to create the Jamawar and Chevron Banarasi sarees.

Tissue brocade weaving uses silk in its warp, and gold or silver *zari* in weft, producing a translucent, shimmering look for the fabric. More silk and *zari* may be used as extra weft for creating designs.

Vasket or Vaskat brocade technique produces an extravagant fabric, with a rich *jaal* (lattice) of traditional patterns in stunning *zari* work. It uses a supplemental *zari* weft throughout the base of the saree, which leaves minimal float on the back of the fabric. Sarees woven in this weaving style are adorned with all-over *zari*, which gives them a rich and lustrous appearance.

Kadiyal or Interlocking technique helps achieve a border in a sharply contrasting color to the rest of the body of the saree, a feat in itself in handloom weaving. This requires careful dyeing and setting the warp in different colors and multiple changes in the weft shuttle while the textile is being woven. This style involves careful consideration and calculation during the weaving process.

Minakari weaving is the textile version of the unmatchable enameling technique by the same name, used in traditional jewelry. This technique is used to enhance miniature motifs in Banarasi weaving with colors and textures, with the painstaking addition of supplementary colored silk threads to the weave in addition to the *zari*. Minakari can be done both in the Kadhuan and Phekwa techniques.

We have seen different types of weaves and fabrics used in Banarasi. The other big variable component is the type of design or pattern used to decorate the saree. Often, it is this design type that is used to identify the saree, for instance, a Jangla or a Tanchoi. Let us now try to understand what some of the more popular design patterns are.

The **Jangla (Jungla)** is a stunning pattern - traditional and opulent. Typical designs include natural motifs of flowers, leaves and vines intricately woven together all along the length of the saree. Often, a wave design (*leher*) is featured, with smaller motifs or *buttis* like a betel leaf or paisley twine, in a dense interlaced pattern. When an elaborate *jaal* (lattice) design is woven all over the saree, it is called as Jangla. The intricacy of the gold *zari* on natural, floral patterns is a captivating feature of a Jangla Banarasi Saree.

The **Jamawar Tanchoi** (also known as just "*Jamewar*") is famous for its rich, vibrant look, its distinctive feature being the paisley motif, intricately interwoven into a colorful silk maze with a texture that makes a delicate, soft drape. The minute motifs are spread out in a dense

yet delicate pattern on the silk base, completely woven into the fabric, in a Tanchoi brocade technique. The *pallu* is often decorated with large paisley motifs. Elegantly rich, butter soft, this is one of the enchanting Banarasi sarees.
The **Shikargah** ("*Shikaar*" means a hunt) is a rich, unique, traditional type, easily identified by designs of hunting scenes, like hunters on horseback or on elephants in pursuit of deer and tigers. Motifs depicting animals, birds, *atifa butti* (an inverted or swaying floral pattern), and jungle scenes make up the design. This type shows a strong Persian influence, with intricate patterns and features like the *jaal* (lattice) on delicately spun textiles.

The fine Kadhuan weave is a hallmark of Banarasi weaving, and cannot be replicated on a powerloom.

The **Rangkat** has a distinctive look with color blocks in the saree in a stripe pattern. It is produced by a very time and labor-intensive weaving technique, where the warp and the weft are intricately woven with multiple sharp changes in colors. The resultant multi-colored pattern is simply spectacular. Incredibly difficult to weave and timeless in its appeal, a Banarasi Rangkat saree is a rare handloom masterpiece and an ultimate indulgence.
The **Valkalam** saree has a simple plain base with a rich woven border and a spectacular *pallu*. Patterns are woven with extra weft in the brocade, typically with soft color combinations of shades from the same family, rather than striking contrasts. The beautiful *resham* work in delicate hues on a soft satin silk base is the hallmark of a classic Banarasi Valkalam drape.

The **Bootidar** is a type with traditional *buttis* (motifs) such as *angoor, gojar, mehrab, paan, ashrafi,* or *chunri butti* woven in the base of the fabric, with magnificent silver arches adorning the border. The combination of gold, silver and silk threads in the weaving give a stunning effect when worn.
The **Banarasi Shalu**, strikingly similar to the acclaimed Paithani, is ubiquitous in Maharashtrian weddings. The fine quality of its silk is embellished with *zari* motifs, beautiful borders and intricately decorated *pallu* forms the hallmark of this type.

It is the different combinations of this wide range of weaves, fabrics and design patterns that give the Banarasi its huge variety. While most of the designs and patterns used in the Banarasi school are its own, it has also embraced influences from other styles, only to further enrich its repertoire, uniqueness and grandeur. Typically, the type of pattern or design gives the saree its generic name, and within this, the weave and fabric are specified to identify a more precise classification. For instance, a Jangla saree can be a Katan silk Jangla Kadhuan or a cotton Jangla Phekwa, based on the fabric and weaving technique used.
Hopefully by now, the complexity of the Banarasi repertoire feels more intuitive to the reader. Yet it is only fair to add here that the patterns described above are but a subset of the variety available. The Banarasi spans such a vast scope of artistry, that it could easily make the topic of a separate book by itself. There is something for every taste here, and irrespective of which Banarasi saree one chooses, it would be a unique piece by itself, steeped in tradition and finessed by centuries of craftsmanship.

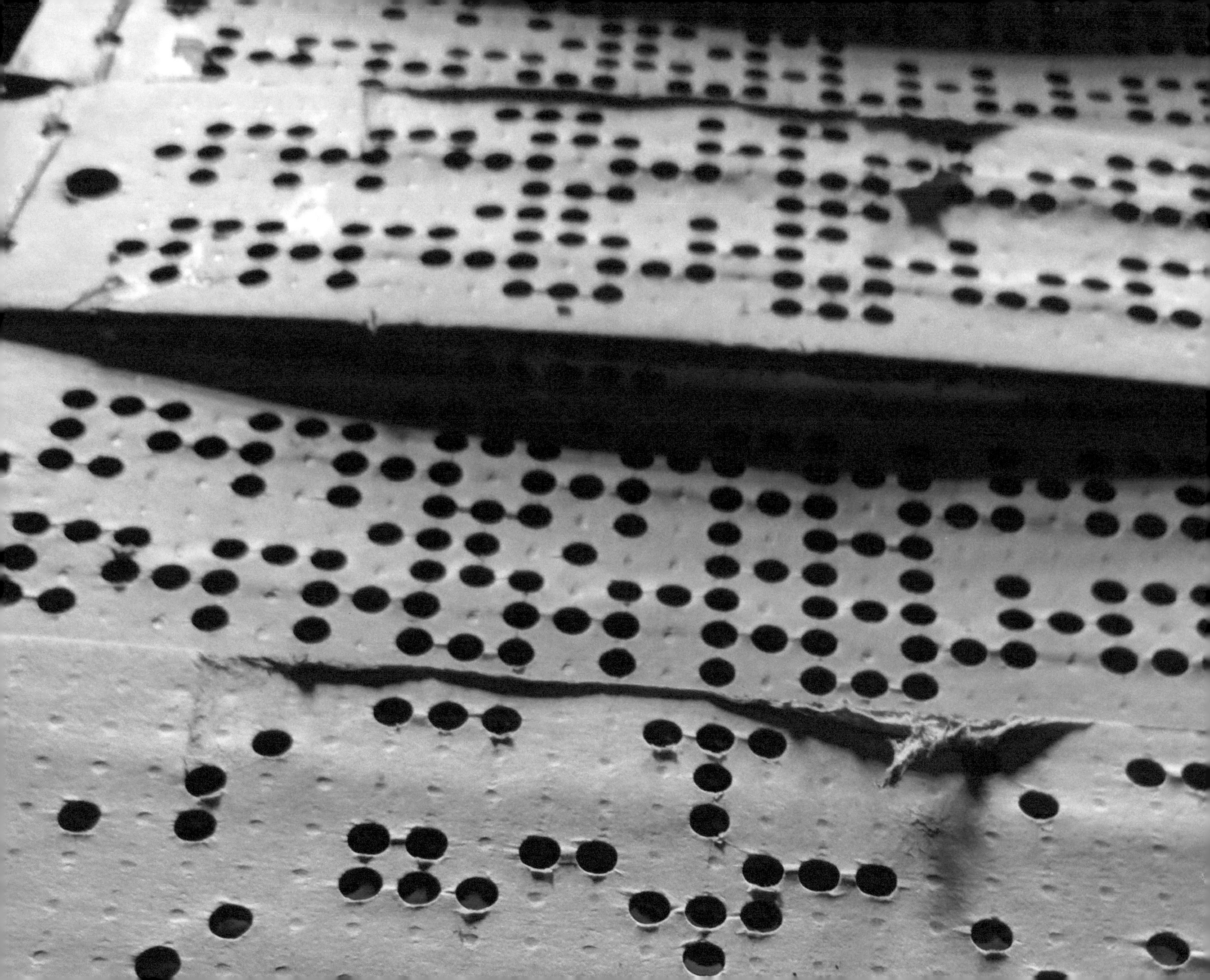

Acknowledgements

This book was conceptualized in late 2019. I knew that realizing this vision would take many different skills and a lot of effort. I reached out to a group of my friends for help. The warm response I received was overwhelming. Twenty-four months later, thanks to the collective team efforts and collaboration of this group across three continents, ten cities, and five countries, the vision was turned into a reality. This book would be incomplete without acknowledging the generous help, good-hearted voluntary efforts and invaluable support I have received from a few people towards putting it together. They have all made my dream possible. I want to share my deepest gratitude to them.

The series of punched cards (see photo on the left page) create patterns on a weaving loom. Similar to those punch cards, this amazing team has created a beautiful book.

To **Haritha Haridas, Medha Nevrekar, Nabarupa Banerjee, Parul Pathak, Rupali Zurale, Sangeeta Wagh, Sejal Desai, Shalmali Patkar-Barve, Shilpa Deshpande, Shobha Sasalatti, Srikala Sivarapu, Vaishali Bhat and Vidya Vasania**, for allowing me to immortalize their exquisite sarees that are featured in this book, and for all their support along the way. I will be eternally grateful to them for entrusting their priceless heirlooms in my care during the photo shoots.

To **Dr. Mrunalini Chavarkar**, for the beautiful work in oil she painted for the book cover. This brilliant masterpiece has created the exact mystique I felt when I began my research on sarees, making for an apt cover for this book. The painting was inspired by the work "Sitting Lady" by artist Mr. Shashikant Dhotre from Maharashtra, India. Thanks, **Shashikant Dhotre**, for giving me permission to use it for the reproduction that adorns the cover.

To **Nabarupa Banerjee**, for readily accepting to be in front of the camera to graciously portray the classic persona of the Bengali beauties through your soft smile, bright eyes and charming personality.
To **Medha Nevrekar**, from DesiAlmaree.com for sharing the artisan work she had photographed, contributing to the weaving process visuals described in the book.

To **Zenobia Davar** from ZenobiaDavar.com, for generously sharing some of her personal family photographs for the book. The masterful craftsmanship of her and her team is evident in the intricately hand-embroidered in multicolored french knots with pure silk skeins decorating the extraordinarily delicate Gara saree featured in this book. I am honored to be able to include this authentic Gara saree with its design of colorful rainforest parrots like cockatoos, lovebirds and macaws from all over the world.

To **Dheer Shah**, for helping me understand what it takes to print a book. His guidance on choosing the right paper, ensuring the right resolution for photographs and the excellent service he provided throughout the project helped me get this book out into the world .

To **Mike Day** from JP-Graphics, for giving the tour of their state-of-the-art printing press and enthusiastically sharing insightful tips on printing techniques.

To **Amy Reilly**, for meticulously proofreading the book.

Top row, from left to right: Zenobia Davar, Vidya Vasania, Srikala Sivarapu, Vaishali Bhat, Somesh Sasalatti
Middle row, from left to right: Shobha Sasalatti, Haritha Haridas, Shalmali Patkar Barve, Sejal Desai, Sangeeta Wagh, Rupali Zurale, Rajiv Thanawala
Bottom row, from left to right: Parul Pathak, Nathan Sivarapu, Medha Nevrekar, Dheer Shah, Nabarupa Banerjee, Mrunalini Chavarkar, and Shilpa Deshpande

To my **photographers, Haritha Haridas, Medha Nevrekar, Nathan Sivarapu, Rajiv Thanawala, Rupali Zurale, Sangeeta Wagh, Shalmali Patkar-Barve, Somesh Sasalatti & Vaishali Bhat**, for the beautiful pictures they created of the sarees featured in this book. They agreed to go on a fun ride with me, where we let our imagination go wild on visualizing different ways to capture these beautiful sarees in print. We had a lot of fun working together, and I enjoyed our discussions about finding the right props to pair with the different sarees. This team worked tirelessly, patiently heeding my never-ending requirements. A few unexpected weather issues added to the challenges of our outdoor photoshoot, but this team used them creatively to give a surprise twist to the pictures, making the results even more brilliant. I cannot describe how difficult it was for me to choose the best among all the fantastic photographs they clicked. Thanks to each one of them for their amazing enthusiasm and creative ideation in translating virtual visuals I had only imagined, into the real and really spectacular visual treat on display in the book.

To **Shilpa Deshpande**, my **book designer**, for converting all the content into an aesthetically pleasing book. Her design skills never cease to amaze me. She taught me book design concepts, starting from the very basic ones, such as the importance of white spaces. From determining the size and dimensions of the book to the small-scale, flip-book she made as the early prototype, she has led the entire layout planning, designing each and every frame beautifully. Her perseverance for always keeping the reader's perspective in mind has led to aesthetically pleasing design elements that the reader can experience throughout the book. I will always be thankful to her for this work and her guidance in making this beautiful book.

To **Vaishali Bhat**, my **editor**. Her voice is reflected in every word and in every line of this book. I present this book to you with greater confidence because of the wonderful editorial work she has done. Vaishali would fully understand and internalize my content and story, digging into its details. Sometimes, she would get me to re-write drafts, pushing me to re-think the rationale. And then she would organize and reorganize the content, picking the right words, moulding sentence structures, toiling for hours on every article. Her superb editing has not only distilled the information to make the most impactful pieces stand out, but has also led to high quality writing that will keep the reader's interest alive despite the primarily informational nature of the content. I thank her for re-defining excellence for me, helping to make this book reader-worthy. Any misses that remain are my own, likely introduced after her careful examination.

Above all, to my wonderful family for their unconditional love, unending patience, unflinching faith and unwavering support that made it possible for me to achieve this daunting task.

I feel truly blessed!

Making a saree

In order to help you, I've laid out some basics in this section, to provide better understanding on the terms used in the saree making process, sprinkled inside the book. When a saree is woven, the most important and complicated part of the whole process is weaving it.

Design Making:
It starts with **pattern designing**. Then with each element of the pattern in mind, careful decisions are made, from choosing the individual colors for the design, to identifying the right raw material for the yarn. After several iterations and engaging discussions between the design team and the weavers, a beautiful saree design emerges.

The **weaving process** then involves several stages in order to produce a lovely saree. Traditionally the process includes preparing the right density yarn, reeling, dyeing, assembling the warp & weft as per the master weaver's design instructions and finally skillfully weaving it on the setup loom.

Yarn: Yarn is a long continuous length of interlocked fibers. The raw material of cotton, silk, wool, or linen, is gently rolled with palm to form a loosely interlocked cylindrical bunch known as a sliver. This loosely interlocked sliver is then spun on a spinning wheel (*charkha*) to make it compact and fine.

A plied yarn is one where multiple strands of yarn — already spun yarn — are put together and twisted in the opposite direction from that in which they were first twisted. A 2-ply yarn has two strands; a 3-ply yarn has three & so on. Any time you ply your yarn, you're making it stronger, as a twist adds strength.

Reeling: In the process of reeling (tying the yarn in a bundle), the threads are separately mounted on the reeling machine, for the warp the yarn is rolled on a shuttle (*dharki*). The yarn for weft is firstly mounted on a charkha and then rolled on the bobbin.

Dyeing is a process of coloring the greige yarns. Dyeing of yarn in a particular color usually involves immersing the reel or cheese of yarn in the dyeing tank. This process is done by hand in small lots or hanks using natural or chemical colorants.

Warp and Weft: Weaving is a method of textile production in which two distinct sets of yarns or threads are interlaced at right angles to form

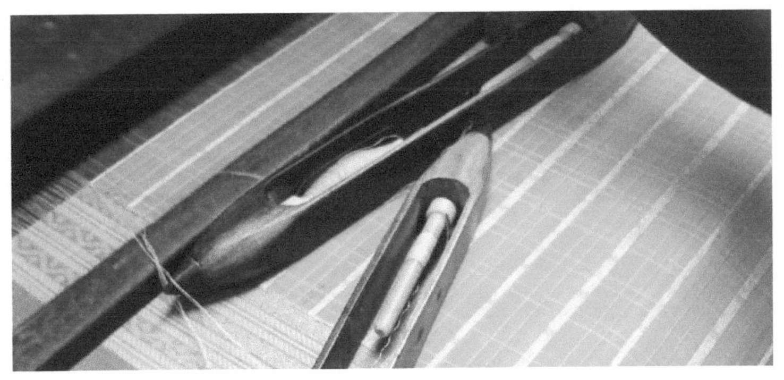

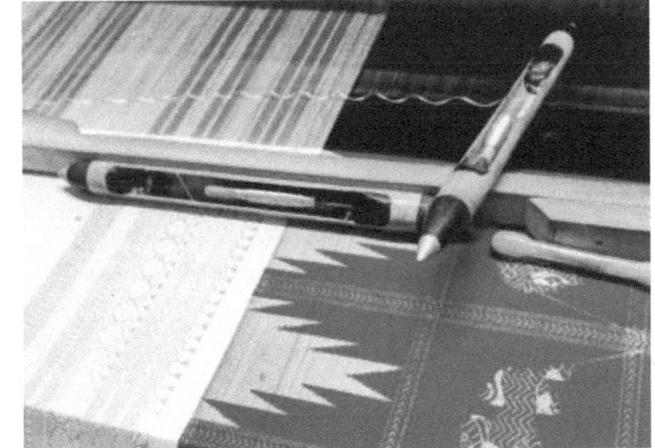

a fabric or cloth. Warp and weft are the two basic components used in weaving to turn thread or yarn into fabric. The lengthwise or longitudinal **warp** (*tana*) yarns are held taut and in parallel to each other, stationary on a frame or loom. The **weft** (*bana*), the latitudinal threads, are placed in a shuttle. As the shuttle moves back and forth when warp yarn is alternately lifted up, the warp and weft threads are interwoven. A single thread of the weft crossing the warp is called a pick.

Looms: A loom is a device used to weave a fabric. There are two main kinds of looms used today: a manual (handloom) and an electric (powerloom). Weaving is a vibrant part of Indian history, and the manual, labor intensive, handloom is still widely used in India today to create sustainably handwoven fabrics. The fabrics which are weaved on handlooms are known as handloom products. As the name suggests, handloom is a loom that is used to weave fabrics using hands, that is, without the use of electricity. The foot pedals are pressed to lift the respective heddles according to the weave plan and it has to be in sync with throwing the weft across the two sections of warp yarns. Depending on the saree types, and the aesthetic design patterns in it, sarees are generally woven on a Dobby, or a Jacquard, or a Pit loom.

Dobby is a type of floor loom that controls the warp yarns in groups, using a harness device called a dobby. When a harness goes up or down, all the warp yarns attached to it move with it. That, combined with the loom only being able to hold a certain number of harnesses limits how complex a pattern can be. Dobby looms are best used for simple geometric patterns based on the limitations of the harnesses.

In **Jacquard** loom, the weaving design stencils are punched into metal or heavy cardboard punch cards that are laced together and fed into the loom to control the woven pattern. The cards collectively form the mechanism to lift the necessary yarns during the process to weave a motif and help translate the pattern in the fabric. Jacquard looms allow for large, intricate designs like elaborate floral or complex patterns, resulting in beautifully woven craftsmanship.

Pit looms are also known as a treadle-loom as it uses treadles to operate the heddle shafts. The treadle loom usually sits close to the ground. The pedals (treadles), which the weaver uses to operate the heddle shafts, sit in a pit and the weaver sits on the ground, hanging his/her legs in the pit to operate the pedals.

References

Alphabetically by Saree Names

Baluchari
Directorate of Textiles, Handlooms, Spinning Mills, Silk Weaving & Handloom Based Handicrafts Division/
https://bengalhandlooms.com/articles/

Banarasi
https://www.tilfi.com/pages/techniques
https://www.holyweaves.com/blogs/the-textiles-blog
https://www.innfinity.in/fashion/types-of-banarasi-sarees/

Bandhani
Bandhani - Rajasthan Industries
http://www.rajasthantextiles.com/bandhani.htm
History of Bandhani or Indian Tie & Dye Technique

Bomkai
The Glorious Odissi Sari
Kalamandir :: Oddissi Sarees
Bomkai Silk

Dharwad Kasuti
Everything About Kasuti Embroidery: Unique Motifs, Its Background And More

Gadwal
http://www.andhraportal.org/gadwal-sarees/
http://gadwal-info.blogspot.com/2007/10/gadwal-complete-information.html
Mirabilis jalapa

Gara
Gara Sari Page 1. Fashion & a Fusion of Cultures From Along the Silk Roads
The Glory of the Gara
Sari sorority: Why Parsi ladies are a fashion treasure
Power dressing: Exhibition-cum-sale of Indira Gandhi inspired saris

Ilkal
https://www.slideshare.net/NanduriAsha/ilkal-saree-by-nanduri-asha
https://www.sarisafari.com/tour/ilkal.html

Jamdani
Soft Dhakai Jamdani sarees
https://www.vogue.in/content/jamdani-saree-history-origin-technique-indian-handloom

Kalamkari
http://www.lepakshihandicrafts.gov.in/category-Machilipatnam-blockprints.html
https://www.faridagupta.com/blog/everything-about-kalamkari-prints.html
http://www.indiamarks.com/kalamkari-the-ancient-indian-art-organic-fabric-painting/

Kanjivaram
Kanjivaram Sarees & their long lost history! | The 6 Yard Love!
https://kanakavalli.com/blogs/kanakavalli-varna-sutra
https://www.sundarisilks.com/blogs/article/kanchipuram-silk-gods-own-silk

Kasavu
https://www.culturalindia.net/indian-dance/classical/mohiniattam.html
http://www.caleidoscope.in/art-culture/handlooms-of-kerala-holding-on-to-the-flag-of-tradition
Kasavukada - South India's Largest Handloom Entrepreneur
Kerala Piravi: History of the simple yet rich Kerala kasavu sari

The Pashmina
http://www.kashmir-rose.com/embroidery
https://www.kashmirbox.com/blog/the-classical-craft-of-kashmiri-tilla-dozi
https://ahujasons.com/exquisite-kaani-weaves-of-the-valley/

Kota
http://travelsintextiles.com/kota-doria/
https://pulpypapaya.com/blog/kota-doria-handwoven-sarees/
http://kotadoriyasaree.com/process/

Kunbi
Riding The Weaves: Meet one of the last remaining kunbi weavers in Goa
Reviving the Kunbi
The Kunbi's niche revival
A dance that revived a sari
Reviving Forgotten Treasures

Madhubani
Madhubani Painting, Mithila Painting, Madhubani Art
http://www.colorofindia.com/madhubani-art.htm

Maheshwari
A Handbook on Maheshwar Handlooms Cluster
The Weaving Story of Maheshwari Saris | Madhya Pradesh

Mysore Silk
http://www.caleidoscope.in/art-culture/fable-of-a-fabulous-fabric-mysore-silk
https://www.ksicsilk.com/

Narayanpet
http://narayanpet.telanganaonline.in/city-guide/about-narayanpet
http://www.telanganatourism.gov.in/partials/about/arts-crafts/narayanpet-handlooms.html

Paithani
Paithani Saree - History, Material, Colour, weaving, motifs of Paithani Saree
Textiles - Paithani weaves of Maharashtra
History of Paithani Sarees | paithani1
Paithani Saree - Paithani Sari, Paithani Sarees, Paithani Silk Saree Maharashtra India

Patola-Pochampally
All About the enchanting Ikat
History - Patan Patola
Pochampalli Handlooms - Telangana Tourism
Pochampally Sarees Take Wings! - The Financial Express

Additional resources
https://textilesofindia.in/glossary/
http://en.wikipedia.org
https://strandofsilk.com/journey-map
http://www.handlooms.in
westbengalhandloom.org
https://www.craftsvilla.com/blog
http://gaatha.com/
utsavpedia.com

CPSIA information can be obtained
at www.ICGtesting.com
Printed in the USA
BVHW010221100223
658265BV00011B/327

* 9 7 8 0 5 7 8 2 8 9 5 4 0 *